TOMA

Hideous Kinky

Hideous Kinky

A screenplay by Billy MacKinnon

Based on the novel by Esther Freud

SCREENPRESS BOOKS

Developed with the support of the European Script Fund, an initiative of the Media Programme of the European Union.

First published in 1999
by ScreenPress Books
28 Castle Street Eye Suffolk IP23 7AW

Photoset by Parker Typesetting Service, Leicester
Printed in England by Clays Ltd, St Ives plc

Hideous Kinky screenplay written by Billy MacKinnon
based on the novel of the same name written by Esther Freud

Billy MacKinnon is hereby identified as author of this
work in accordance with Section 77 of the Copyright,
Designs and Patents Act 1988

A CIP record for this book
is available from the British Library

ISBN I 901680 25 8

For more information on forthcoming ScreenPress Books,
contact the publishers at:

ScreenPress Books
28 Castle Street
Eye Suffolk
IP23 7AW
fax on: 01379 870 267
e.mail on: screenpressbooks@hotmail.com

10 9 8 7 6 5 4 3 2 1

for Sophie

Contents

Foreword

I was a long haired kid in Marrakech in 1972. I was back again in 1976, this time for six months, much of that time spent in the Sahara. Just as it had felt personally relevant that my brother, Billy, and I should make *Small Faces*, set in our home city of Glasgow in 1968, so it felt natural that I would direct Billy's screenplay of *Hideous Kinky*, from Esther Freud's novel.

It was great to be back in the dust and colour of Morocco. As usual, I had a notebook with me at all times and it soon filled up with rapidly drawn thumbnail sketches – anything which might later be reproduced to detail crowd scenes or to place in an empty landscape.

Kate Winslet was my first choice to play Julia. I was aware of a certain courage in her acting which was what the character required. Before we knew it, she had joined us in Morocco for the pre-production location recee. This must be a first, the star of the film travelling around the countryside with the crew, a month before shooting was due to begin.

I had seen Saïd Taghmaoui in *La Haine* and I thought he was brilliant. We needed someone to play Bilal who had a strong personality and wouldn't end up being a shadow of Kate. Born in

people - in shade of tree

Paris, Saïd's parents were Moroccan Berbers, so this role had a special meaning for him.

The children, Carrie Mullan and Bella Riza, were found after extensive casting by Suzie Figgis. They were both eight years old and we were concerned about their ability to adjust both to Moroccan life and the shooting schedule. The first rehearsal in a Moroccan hotel resulted in fifty minutes of tears, followed by an excellent ten minutes of work. But they soon came to enjoy their new extended family – the film crew.

Mats propped up with stick for tent

We had a British and Moroccan crew working side by side. Apart from the British catering, which didn't go down too well with the Moroccans, it all worked rather harmoniously. The Moroccans were accustomed to their country being used as a stand-in for other places – Tibet, Jerusalem etc. – so it meant a lot to them that this was a film about Morocco – some of them even remembered the original Freud family whose adventures inspired the story.

All three of the Freuds turned up in Marrakech. I recall with pleasure strolling around the medina with Esther and Bella as they identified their old childhood haunts – 'Hey! That's the cafe we used to run around shouting "Hideous Kinky!"'

The greatest task was to reproduce the medina, as it wasn't possible to base ourselves there for the shoot. We constructed our own medina in the square of a Berber village. We identified everyone and everything we needed – musicians, story tellers, medicine men, animals, shops – and bussed the lot onto our own set, where we could have near total control. This enabled us to keep abreast of the schedule without too many unpredictable situations.

The few times we did shoot inside the medina, things got a little out of hand. It is almost impossible to pay off a street of Moroccan shopkeepers because there is never a finite number, and the ones who haven't been paid all turn out to be cobblers who bash hammers whenever they hear the word 'Action'.

We wanted a film with its own distinctive rhythm to conjure up Marrakech in 1972. It was a time of optimism and a certain innocence.

Gillies MacKinnon
December 1998

Hideous Kinky

EXT. MARRAKECH. DAY

The Medina – the walled heart – of an ancient Arab city. Late afternoon. Business has reopened for the day. Daylight leans in great wedges of light and dark into the town, while in the narrow lanes and catacombs night is already gathering. This is the hour when the Medina disgorges its inhabitants: veiled women with their children, merchants, criers, shoppers, idlers, beggars, handcarts, mangy animals. From every corner the primitive loudspeakers sing of the Prophet or the desert as, in a dusty chorus of bells and horns, the cars and bicycles crawl through the pedestrian mire.

EXT. MARRAKECH. DAY

Backs and the backs of heads and hands; a hanging pointed hood and its tassel; brown ankles in yellow slippers, feet in thonged sandals and feet clad only in dust. A cartwheel trundles by and a small dark infant is borne aloft on shoulders against the sky. A group of eyes look round and down. Darting and weaving, dashing clear, engulfed again in this tide of shapes – a small girl lost in the crowd.

EXT MARRAKECH. DAY

We catch the girl in detail now. She is six years old, though small – perhaps – for her age. She wears a dusty Arab kaftan, almost ragged; there are English schoolgirl's pigtails held by ribbons on either side of her head; on her feet, a pair of battered Clarks

I

sandals. Her complexion is light, made up of pinks and creams, and her grey eyes are – for now – wide and wild with terror. This is Lucy.

EXT. MARRAKECH. DAY

Crying her eyes out, Lucy makes her way down a lane of carpet sellers.

EXT. MARRAKECH. DAY

Down a narrower, darker lane, a black tunnel leads to a tiny half-disc of late-afternoon light. Cloaked figures with pointed hoods on their heads move there. With a little cry, she doubles back towards the congested main street.

EXT. MARRAKECH. DAY

An Arab woman leans and extends her arms towards the frightened little girl. The woman's face is veiled; only her eyes can be seen. Lucy screams, rooted to the spot.

EXT. MARRAKECH. DAY

Now Lucy dashes into the middle of a large square. Here there are handcarts, animals, great crowds. She shuts her eyes, her face in a grimace, screaming as she runs, just a blind welter of tears and panic.

LUCY

Mum-mee!!

Heads turn. A man approaches.

Mum-meeeeee!!

INT. HOTEL ROOM. DAWN

A young woman wakes and sits upright on her mattress. Thick hair tumbles from her shoulders, almost to her waist. This is Julia.

3

The hotel room is quiet and all but dark. Only a small window, high on the furthest wall, gives out a pale oblong of pre-dawn light.

Julia looks to the mattress opposite. Lying there is Lucy. Next to her, asleep, is her sister, eight-year-old Bea. Lucy's eyes are open and bright in the half-light.

> JULIA
> (*whispers*)

Lucy?

> LUCY

Mum?

Julia smiles with affection and secret relief.

Is it Christmas yet?

> JULIA

No, darling. Not till morning.

> LUCY

Is it morning yet?

Julia looks at her two daughters. Lucy looks back.

> JULIA

OK. Come on.

Julia uncovers a side of the mattress and Lucy crosses the room and snuggles in beside her.

Happy?

> LUCY

Hideous . . .

EXT. MARRAKECH. DAWN

From some distant point in the city, a muezzin starts the prayer for dawn. The song is slow, liquid and melodious. Marrakech in half-light.

4

Fade to black, then music up.

Credit up: HIDEOUS KINKY.

INT. HOTEL. DAY

Morning and the hotel has woken up. Sunshine streams through the central skylight into the courtyard below, illuminating the landings with their numerous doors, the washing hung from every banister, the to and fro of children and adults. A radio plays.

Title: MARRAKECH. 1972.

Julia stands in a queue for the landing's single toilet, a big red and white striped towel in her arms. Bea and Lucy emerge from the toilet together and approach her.

On the landing above, a woman in a purple kaftan sits on a spacious planter's chair. Another, in green, leans with an elbow against the railing. Both seem heavily made-up and great henna-red manes of hair extend down their backs. A man stands opposite the green one, smoking a cigarette, raffish in black baggy pants and a white shirt. They notice the two girls on the landing below. These are the Henna Ladies.

> FIRST HENNA LADY

Hello, darling!

> SECOND HENNA LADY
> (*from her seat*)

Hi!

Lucy and Bea smile up.

> LUCY

Merry Christmas!

The women laugh. Julia looks up at them.

5

JULIA

No, darling, not in Morocco it isn't. Every week a new set of men. Have you noticed?

BEA

Prostitutes.

JULIA
(*still looking up*)

Do you think so?

Then she looks at Bea.

Where did you learn that?

But Bea has already made off down the landing, with Lucy behind. The two girls descend a stairwell.

BEA
(*off*)

Bugger, bastard and bum!

LUCY
(*off*)

Bugger, bastard, bum!

JULIA

Hey!

BEA
(*off*)

Hideous Kinky!

INT. HOTEL ROOM. DAY

Julia has set a little stool beside the wardrobe and she reaches up and brings down a large brown parcel. Now all three sit on the floor with the half-opened package between them. Julia reaches in and removes a first small packet, the girls' eyes following her every move. She looks at it.

JULIA

What's this?

(*she opens it*)

Party hats. How useful.

Now she withdraws a woman's shirt, unfolds it and hold it at arm's length. It is a lime green tunic with rough embroidery in black and purple. It seems to please her. She sniffs it.

King's Road.

Julia lays the tunic flat on the floor and Bea begins to inspect it. Now Julia removes a pair of boy's small boxing gloves in red leather. A smile flickers on her lips.

Another joke . . .

Julia brings out a dark jar with a label hanging from it.

Italian truffles. How gross. Well, at least they're edible.

Julia's hands are back in the parcel. Now she has a small brown envelope. The girls watch her as she looks at it quizzically, then opens it.

Two tickets to the Royal Albert Hall on 1 January?

BEA

Mum . . .

Julia holds up a small football shirt in the colours of Manchester United. A big number '1' in white has been stitched to the front of it. She looks at the girls.

Mum . . . it's the wrong parcel.

JULIA

But it's addressed. Look. It's definitely for us.

BEA

It's for 'Bloody Mandy', isn't it? And that 'boy'.

                              LUCY
    Mum, where's our presents?

                               BEA
    Kensington, I expect. If theirs are here.

*Stunned, Julia looks at the wall. Finally, another envelope emerges
from the bag. She opens it and reads the card inside.*

                              JULIA
    'My darlings Mandy and Lionel' . . .

She crumples the card.

    Darlings! *Lionel!* Your bloody father . . .

*The girls just watch her. Julia's eyes take in the room – its
meanness – with the two mattresses on the floor, the piles of
clothes, the squat clay stove with its pots and pans. Her glance
lights on the primitive alarm clock. She turns back to the girls and
sighs, and a tear rolls down her cheek.*

*Lucy and Bea present Julia with an orange and a pear, and push
them across the floor.*

                              LUCY
    Happy Christmas, Mum.

EXT. MARRAKECH. DAY

*A bright-green fez surmounts a dark face: sunglasses, cheeks like
bellows. Two sets of fingers flick and buzz along the length of a
wailing Moroccan oboe.*

*A dozen Berber horsemen stand in a line, their horses bedecked in
red and powerfully kicking up dust. In unison, the men raise their
muskets. Gunshots rend the air.*

*Lucy and Bea wince at the sudden report. They are standing in
front of Julia, barefoot and in kaftans, with their paper hats on
their heads.*

EXT. COMMUNE. DAY

We are in a room in Marrakech: mattresses everywhere, sleeping bags, a guitar being inexpertly played. Two young men sit with their backs to the wall, their knees up to their chins. There is a girl next to one of them, smoking a joint, and Julia is next to her. Lucy is on her lap and Bea is drawing on the floor. To the side and back, three teenage hippies make stew on a small paraffin stove. One of the young men, Greg, an American, speaks.

> GREG
>
> This kid's father's a poet, right?

> JULIA
>
> In London.

> GREG
>
> That's cool.

He indicates to Julia the straggly-haired boy next to him.

> This is Frank.

> FRANK
> (*spacy, grinning*)
>
> Hi . . .

> GREG
>
> From Frankfurt.

> FRANK
>
> Hi . . .

> GREG
>
> Frank brought three hundred trips from Frankfurt, didn't he? Right there in his backpack. Took them to Diabet. Laid them on the entire village.

> FRANK
>
> Hey . . .

GREG

Hippies, freaks, Moroccans. Man, woman and child. LSD.
Pure. Three hundred tabs.

(*chuckles*)

Man. Woman. And child. Oh, man . . .

He looks at Frank with undisguised respect.

Lucy goes to drink from a metal tumbler.

FRANK

Hey . . .

JULIA

I don't think so, darling.

*A veiled woman appears in the doorway and enters. Undoing her
headscarf and veil, she reveals a smiling, pretty Swedish-blonde
face. This is Eva.*

Oh, Eva! Oh, hi!

EVA

Hi!

GREG

Hey, Eva . . .

*Eva grimaces, eyeing him with cold hostility. Julia jumps to her
feet. Together they leave the room, the girls following.*

See you there, lady.

INT. COMMUNE. DAY

*The four of them enter a small apartment. A number of African
musical instruments hang on the wall. Eva gestures at the room
and to the two girls to be seated. From downstairs there is still the
indistinct strumming of a guitar and a muffled shout of, 'Oh, man!'*

EVA

So. This is what happens when you leave Stockholm and come

to Morocco for a good time. You get married and become a
Muslim!

Eva leans into a small antechamber.

Adil!

*Adil appears. While Eva is light and pretty, he is black-dark
Moroccan, handsome and sinewy. They are like twins from a fairy-
tale.*

Adil, this is Julia.

ADIL
(*in perfect English*)
I'm very pleased to meet you, Julia.

EVA
Adil has toured all over Europe.

JULIA
(*puts her hand to her heart*)
I've heard your music. I think it's . . .

ADIL
Thank you.

EVA
Unfortunately, people much prefer his somersaults over there.

ADIL
And handstands.

EVA
(*grinning*)
Yes. Adil has done handstands in France, handstands in
Germany, Italy . . .

ADIL
Holland . . . Denmark . . .

EVA

Yes. Where they also deported him!

Eva and Adil break into laughter.

*Eva sits on a backless couch and pats the cushion beside her,
beckoning to Julia to join her. From under the couch, she removes
a slightly battered curly-toed man's leather slipper, wrapped in a
heavy, ornate brocade.*

So here's what you were asking about. The greatest living Sufi
. . . Sheikh Ben Jalil.

*The two women look at the object with a mixture of sorrow and
longing. Beyond that, creeping up unnoticed above their shoulders,
are Bea and Lucy. Their eyes are filled with apprehension and
horror.*

JULIA

Did he give it to you?

EVA

Yes. Sort of.

JULIA

He must have tiny feet.

EVA

The most elegant of old men. And not only a great teacher,
but a true saint.

BEA

In a school?

EVA

Yes . . .
(*smiling at Julia*)
The school of the annihilation of the ego.

She sees Bea's confusion.

To find the God within, Bea.

13

JULIA

Will you show me what he taught you? I'd really love to
know.

Eva shakes her head.

EVA

That would only be a bad impersonation. You will have to go
yourself.

She puts her hand on top of Julia's.

In fact, Julia, I think you must.

EXT. STREET. DAY

*Late afternoon, in failing light. Lucy holds Julia's hand on one
side. Bea walks on the other. Under her free arm, Julia carries the
brocade parcel.*

BEA

Are we going to Algeria, Mum? To see the Sufi?

JULIA

I'd love to. Wouldn't you?

Bea just walks along, looking straight ahead.

But we'll have to make some money first.

BEA

Make money? Oh, that's all right then . . .

EXT. HOTEL COURTYARD. EVENING

*Evening now and all three of them are seated on a small carpet in
the hotel courtyard. The girls eat, watching as Julia spreads out the
beginnings of a rag doll, scissors and cotton to hand.*

BEA

What's the point, Mum?

JULIA

Everyone has to work, Bea.

BEA

But nobody wants them.

*Julia spreads another helping of truffle paste on to bread. She
hands it to Lucy.*

JULIA

Eat it all up, darling.

LUCY

It tastes like mud.

JULIA

It's a delicacy, actually.

LUCY

Mum, when can we have rice pudding again?

JULIA

Very soon. As soon as the cheque comes from your father.

BEA

Sure. Father Xmas.

Julia looks at Bea, her face tense and tired.

LUCY

Don't we want to go home, Mum?

JULIA

You are home, darling.

She strokes Lucy's hair.

Oh, darling, London is cold. Cold and sad. No camel. No
Abdul-the-jellybean. No . . .

BEA

No scorpions.

LUCY

So don't we want to go home?

JULIA

No, Lucy. Not yet.

Julia seems suddenly sad and remote.

Not by a long way.

INT. HOTEL ROOM. NIGHT

Dark now. Julia is asleep on her mattress. On the opposite bed, the two girls are lying face to face, curled into one another. Lucy speaks in a whisper to Bea.

LUCY

When you grow up, would you like to be a shepherd?

BEA

No, I don't think so.

LUCY

What then?

Bea looks over at Julia.

BEA

I don't know. I'd like to be normal, I think.

She smuggles down into the blanket, Lucy with her.

Go on. Go on . . . Once upon a time . . .

LUCY

Once upon a time, there was a big house, all alone in the desert.

Lucy stops and collects herself. From somewhere, too, begins the sound of a lonely, keening wind.

It had a hundred rooms, but they were all empty and no one lived there, not for lifetimes and lifetimes. Then in the last

room in the house, where it was all dark, lived a spooky
carpet.

The keening wind increases, but only Lucy hears it.

Years and years passed, and it lived on the floor and it was
lonely and grumpy, and no one came, only ants and a few
birds, and scorpions lived under it . . .

*The wind sound abruptly stops. We see Lucy's face: she is startled
and has frightened herself.*

                              BEA

And then?

                              LUCY
                          (*distracted*)

Then?

                              BEA

Then one day?

EXT. CITY SQUARE. DAY

*A patch of earth in the city square at midday. Tannoy music and
drums. Distant voices singing. A young man and two little boys
throw a carpet on to the ground. The young man is Bilal. The two
boys are Aziz and Isham.*

*With a puff of dust the carpet lands and they deftly unroll it. Now
we see it spread beneath us, large and richly patterned, but
threadbare too, and here and there caked with dried mud.*

*As if magically, the carpet is now inhabited. A very old man, the
Hadaoui, sits on it cross-legged, wearing a somewhat dusty turban.
In front of him is a smoking waterpipe and around him an
arrangement of little metal pots, each with a bright plastic flower
in it. Bilal walks on his hands around the perimeter of the carpet
and the Hadaoui starts to proclaim. A crowd has gathered.*

Now we see the Hadaoui close to: snaggle-toothed, a face like dark

*parchment. Taking in a deep lungful of kif from his pipe, he speaks
an unbroken monologue in unsubtitled Berber.*

*From a basket, Bilal brings out two doves. With one in each hand,
he throws them – fluttering white – into the air. The doves circle
wide against the clear Marrakech sky. He calls up to them.*

> BILAL
> (*in Arabic*)
> Fatima! Halimah! Return! And bring with you the future. And
> bring with that the truth.

We find Lucy and Bea at the front of the onlookers.

*Bilal flips himself upside-down and begins to wander the carpet on
his hands again. Aziz calls out.*

> AZIZ
> (*in Arabic*)
> And what is the truth?

*Bilal comes to an inverted standstill, his face a sudden blank. Lucy
cranes her neck.*

> BILAL
> (*in Arabic*)
> The truth is a man! Standing upright in the sun!

*He jerkily moves off again. Laughter. The Hadaoui continues his
monologue. Bilal flips back on to his feet. Now the other young
boy speaks.*

> ISHAM
> (*in Arabic*)
> And what is the future?

Bilal goes round the ring of faces, interrogating with his eyes.

> BILAL
> (*in Arabic*)
> Who will answer that? Who has faith? Who has courage? Who?

20

Passing Lucy, he looks down at her, stops, throws her a wink.
Lucy beams. Bilal melts into the crowd. The Hadaoui continues his
monologue.

AZIZ
(*in Arabic, pointing*)

Listen! The Hadaoui knows the truth!

Now Bilal speaks up from the crowd, in a voice not quite his own.

BILAL
(*in Arabic*)

So tell me this, then.

He points behind into the centre of the group and talks over his
shoulder.

Which side of my arse has the boil on it? Tell me that . . .

Laughter. Briefly, the Hadaoui stops his monologue.

HADAOUI

Allah Akbar!

CROWD

Allah Akbar!

BILAL
(*in Arabic*)

No! Then tell me this . . .

With a look of excitement on her face, Lucy makes her way from
the crowd.

EXT. SQUARE. DAY

Julia is some way apart, but we can still see the group of
onlookers. A roar of laughter comes from the crowd. There is a
basket of six multicoloured rag dolls under her arm and she is
trying to sell them.

JULIA

Dolls? Interested? Not interested?

Lucy runs up to Julia. Grabbing her wrist in both hands, she begins to drag her towards the crowd.

Lucy? Lucy, what are you doing?

LUCY

Look, Mum!

In the sky above their heads, the doves are returning.

EXT. SQUARE. DAY

Now Julia is in the crowd, somewhere behind Lucy. Lucy and Bea watch as the Hadaoui speaks.

One dove is perched on the old man's turban. He holds the other bird in his two hands, its beak to his ear. Turning the dove to his face, he quietly interrogates it, then brings it to his ear again. Isham calls out from the crowd.

ISHAM

Hadaoui! What more does the dove say?

The Hadaoui pauses.

HADAOUI

The dove says, 'Greater than all the sands of the world is the number of the souls of men. And each has a destiny, and each has a name, known only to God.'

His eyes go round the crowd.

Now every man must look to his own heart.

AZIZ

Truth is the voice of a bird!

The performance is over. Lucy watches as Bilal stands, and Aziz goes round the crowd gathering coins in a tambourine. Bilal looks once more in her direction and she seizes the opportunity. Running to the perimeter of the carpet, she plucks one of the plastic flowers from its jar and presents it to him. He smiles down at her, relaxed, and accepts the flower with a little bow, happy to keep up the performance. Lucy repeats the action, and then again. The last time, he completes his bow and looks over her head, distracted. She follows his eyeline. He is looking at Julia, who is among the onlookers.

Lucy rushes into the crowd. Julia is in the middle of conversation, but Lucy grabs her by the hand and drags her towards the carpet.

> JULIA

Lucy! Now what!

Lucy continues to pull Julia till they are standing in front of Bilal.

> LUCY

This is my mum.

Bilal touches his chest with his right hand.

> BILAL

Bilal . . . Bilal al Hamal.

> LUCY

Bilal speaks Arabic.

> JULIA
> (*in Arabic*)

Oh . . . How do you do?

> BALIL
> (*in Arabic*)

I am well indeed.

They smile at each other.

And this is your daughter?

> JULIA

I'm sorry. That's as much as I know.

BILAL

And is this your daughter?

He smiles again and Julia smiles meltingly back. Lucy looks up at them, her hand in Julia's. She carefully takes Bilal's hand in her other free one. He doesn't seem to notice.

LUCY
(*to herself, chanting slightly*)
Bilal al Hamal . . . Hamal al Bilal.

EXT. MARKET. DAY

Unaccompanied now, Bea and Lucy go flying through the crowded marketplace, over the terrace of an open-air café and into a nearby square, where they are joined by a ragged group of little beggar girls.

BEGGAR GIRLS
Waah-Bea! Waah-Lucy!

BEA
Waah-Khadija! Waah-Zara!

Together they rush off through the square in a dust storm of shrieks and rags and little legs.

EXT. MARRAKECH. DAY

A crowded side street in the Marrakech Medina. There are Arab salesmen, hustlers, women in veils, the occasional tourist. In the midst of this stands a tall, darkly handsome young Moroccan man in his mid-twenties. His gaze moves through the crowd, his eyes intensely alert. Though he is cheaply dressed in a threadbare cheesecloth shirt, there is pride of appearance here. Still, a closer look might show us that he is wearing a pair of plimsolls that don't match. This is Bilal again.

A European tourist appears in the crowd and Bilal snaps to attention.

BILAL

You are a lucky man!

The man totally ignores him. Eventually, another tourist passes.

You are a lucky man, sir!

The tourist looks round at Bilal, his attention briefly caught. Then his expression turns from curiosity to contempt, and Bilal's voice trails off ineffectually.

Two women love you . . .

Bilal resumes his place in the crowd with a hunted look on his face.

Now a young American woman appears on his side of the pavement. Bilal almost throws himself in her path and we see her more closely: wire-rimmed glasses and cropped short hair; tough and nervy thin.

Madam.

The woman exhales a stream of cigarette smoke.

WOMAN
(*tired, New York accent*)

What?

Bilal gives out his most charming smile.

BILAL

One cigarette . . .

INT. CAFÉ. DAY

A crowded café in Marrakech. Bilal and the American woman sit opposite each other. Reaching over, he takes her tea glass from the table and looks into it, turning it in his hand.

BILAL
There are two women. No. Three women. And a journey.

WOMAN

A journey? How very original.

BILAL

No. And something bad.

Bilal sits there with his head down, maintaining a silence.

WOMAN

Bad? What kind of bad?

He looks at her levelly and speaks under his breath.

BILAL

Ten American dollar . . .

WOMAN

What?

BILAL

Ten American dollar . . .

Crossing her arms, she looks around herself. Now she fixes her gaze on Bilal.

WOMAN

Get lost.

BILAL

No, you must help me to tell you. It is most important.

WOMAN

So maybe you should tell it to the police.

She makes to stand.

BILAL
(*smiles*)

Oh no. Nothing could possibly be that bad.

Raising a flicker of a response from the woman, he gestures her to remain seated.

Please . . .

WOMAN

Well . . .

BILAL

You will . . .

WOMAN

Uh-huh . . .

BILAL

You will never have a husband.

WOMAN

That bad, uh? No husband. My God . . .

BILAL

I am sorry. It is best to know such things.

The woman breaks into laughter.

It is of value, no?

She stands.

WOMAN

You complete . . . loser . . .

Bilal watches quizzically as a coin rings on the tabletop and the woman exits. For a moment he sits dejectedly.

EXT. MEDINA. EVENING

Bilal moves down a narrow street in the Medina. To the side is the entrance to a lane. Hearing voices there, he stops. In fact it is a terrible fracas of half a dozen Arab women. Julia is in the centre of it, and one of the women is trying to wrench Julia's basket from her arms. Bilal rushes into the group. We notice three of the women have babies tied to their backs.

BILAL
(*in Arabic*)
Stop! Stop!

The group parts, but one of the women approaches and raises a closed fist as if to strike him. He speaks again, calmly and very quietly.

What are you doing?

The woman lowers her hand, then suddenly grabs Julia's basket and marches to the mouth of the lane. Julia goes to restrain her, but Bilal touches her arm.

No . . .

The dolls fly on to the pavement and the basket rolls across the street.

FIERCE WOMAN
(*in Arabic*)
Nobody wants these things! They are an offence to God! Monstrosities!

Bilal leads Julia past the group and out of the lane.

SECOND WOMAN
(*in Arabic*)
Tell her. This is our street. Do her business somewhere else.

FIERCE WOMAN
(*in Arabic*)
Like the bottom of the sea . . .

The women leave. Bilal retrieves the basket, then kneels beside Julia, who is picking up the dolls.

JULIA
Why are they so angry?

BILAL
They are not angry. They are just . . . poor.

28

They look at each other.

You are a lucky woman, madam!

They beam and laugh, pleased with each other's company.

EXT. BUILDING SITE. DAY

A donkey laden on either flank with baskets full of earth; a rambling scaffold made of rope and wood; an endless chain of human labour carrying sacks of rocks on their shoulders. This is a Moroccan quarry. Down a steep, dusty slope clamber Aziz and Isham. They carry heavy petrol cans full of water in each hand. The two boys join the group.

Among the gang of labourers we recognize Bilal – but only just, as he looks like a ghost, covered from head to foot with white dust.

EXT. STREET. DAY

Bilal, dirty from work, walks down the narrow lanes of the Medina.

Keeping their distance, Lucy and Bea fall quietly in behind him.

INT. BILLET. DAY

A narrow, mean lane and an archway into a wall. Bea and Lucy follow Bilal in. They find an earth floor and, lit by three or four pale light bulbs, a chill windowless corridor extending into infinite darkness. On either side are rows of metal beds, rags, scant personal effects. Dozens of men sit, or sleep, or huddle clustered over playing cards.

Bea and Lucy grow fearful of this place, then they suddenly see Bilal and Julia together. The girls start in surprise. Now the adults notice them.

JULIA

Bea? Lucy?

BEA and LUCY

Mum?

BILAL

This is my house. And these are my brothers.

He gestures at the space.

All forty of them . . .

EXT. SQUARE. NIGHT

*Bea and Lucy are in the square with Eva. Dressed in a shabby
robe, a smiling old man plays an African guitar.*

EXT. SQUARE. NIGHT

*In another part of the square, Julia and Bilal are seated on a bench.
In the rush and buzz of the crowd, a kind of stillness hangs
between them. Julia tenses her mouth, then, like an explosion:*

JULIA

Lichow foo gridoo!

BILAL

Lichow foo gridoo? Ashnawahada? N'chowfoordu . . .

JULIA

N'chowfoordu . . . N'chowfoordu . . .

BILAL
(*rolling his tongue*)

Rrrrrr, Julia, rrrr . . .

Julia joins in, her eyes in his.

JULIA

Rrrrrr . . .

BILAL
(*quietly*)

Parfait . . .

EXT. COURTYARD. DAY

Down in the courtyard, Bea and Lucy play a noisy game of Hideous Kinky tag.

INT. HOTEL ROOM. DAY

Morning light comes through the window. Julia's head is on the pillow and strands of her hair fall over her face. Asleep in the soft light, she looks even younger than usual, beautiful. A dark hand comes and gently moves aside the fallen hair. It is Bilal's, and his face is on the pillow next to her.

He slides up close, about to kiss her, his hand travelling down her back, then front, opening her shirt. She stirs and turns, a faint, sleepy smile on her face. His smile, in turn, is full of tenderness, his eyes intently on hers. Then, out of nowhere, a little finger taps his bare shoulder.

He turns his head to find Lucy lying under the blanket on the other side of him. He smiles, softly surprised.

                         LUCY
     Are you pleased to see me?

INT. HOTEL ROOM. DAY

The hotel is awake now, and voices and footsteps and muffled radio sounds enter from the open door. Bilal is by the doorway, lighting the clay stove.

Julia enters with a bowl of steaming water in her hands. She crouches beside Bilal and unpeels his T-shirt. We see his back is covered in raw, red welts.

                         BILAL
     It is only caused by the dust.

Julia begins to bathe his sores.

JULIA

They work you like animals.

Bilal winces.

BILAL

This is not England, Julia.

He looks at the girls.

Their father. He is a bad man?

JULIA

No. Not bad. Just kind of . . . forgetful.

BILAL

So he is a hippy?

JULIA

Not exactly. More of a writer and a poet. A good one in fact. Quite famous.

BILAL

Then he is rich?

JULIA

Well . . . sometimes.

BILAL

But you left him.

JULIA

Rather than share him, yes.

BILAL

Then he has other wives and children.

JULIA

Not wives exactly, no . . .

Balil thinks about this.

I need things for myself, Bilal.

34

She indicates the girls.

And I need things for them.

BILAL

Things . . .

JULIA

Things like a different life. Something different from before.

She puts her lips to his shoulder.

Things like you.

Bea and Lucy approach him.

BEA

Lucy has made up a song for you. Do you want to hear it?

Lucy, suddenly shy, hides behind her older sister.

LUCY

Maybe tomorrow.

BEA

And maybe for money!

Bilal smiles at them.

BILAL

Very good.

He stands and their eyes follow him.

But that is not how you make money.

He bends into a crouch, then, in front of the two astonished girls, throws a perfect backward somersault, landing with a dull thud of bare feet on the kitchen floor.

This is how to make money!

EXT. COURTYARD. DAY

In harsh sunlight an empty, walled courtyard made of dust and rubble. Bilal enters frame, walking on his hands. With a double backflip, he lands upright on his feet.

Bea and Lucy follow and lay out a small Arab rug.

Now we see Lucy, taut and still, in a perfect handstand.

BILAL

That is excellent . . .

Except we now see that Bilal is holding her by the ankles. He no sooner lets her go than she collapses straight on to the crown of her head. She sits there, rubbing her scalp.

Now it is Bea's turn. Bilal squats beside her encouragingly. She holds the pose for just a second more, then topples, feet flailing, and her heel clips Bilal on the corner of his eye. Lucy's hand flies to her mouth. Bilal cradles his eye.

No problem. No problem.

Now Lucy and Bea perform an identically hopeless cartwheel that leaves them spread-eagled on the rug.

Now they are doing leapfrog on the rug, their eyes on Bilal the whole time to see if he is impressed.

Yes, but . . .

BEA

Of course. Anyone can do that.

Now Lucy is alone on the rug. One hand holds an upraised ankle, while the other secures a cardboard fez to her head, and she is hopping on the spot on one leg. Bilal and Bea watch, smilingly unimpressed.

Now it is Bilal, juggling five oranges with stunning dexterity. In fact he's gone from despair to sheer boredom and is showing off. The girls look up at him utterly discouraged.

No?

Their faces answer him.

Well, I suppose it takes work.

He squats on the ground next to them.

Perhaps we start with something easy.

He takes a matchbox from his pocket.

Watch carefully.

He lights the match, then puts it in his mouth, extinguishing it. The girls just look at him with utter horror on their faces.

Rising to his feet, Bilal bursts out in a peal of laughter and ruffles Lucy's hair.

We'll try again tomorrow.

Bea moves to the far end of the courtyard, gathering the fallen oranges. Lucy watches her go.

LUCY

Bilal?

Bilal looks down at her.

LUCY

If you said something, would it always be the truth?

BILAL

What? Yes. Always . . .

LUCY

And if you promised to do something, would you always do it?

Bilal smiles at her, but his eyes look shifty.

BILAL

Of course.

He looks back to where Bea is.

LUCY

Bilal?

Bilal puts his hands on his knees and bends towards her. She doesn't instantly speak, but also seems to have half an eye on Bea. Bilal gives a gentle shake of his head: what?

Now Lucy squints up at him in the hard afternoon sunlight. She whispers:

Are you my daddy now?

INT. HOTEL ROOM. NIGHT

Bea is winding Lucy's head with a long turban cloth that extends the whole length of the room, from their corner to the doorway. Bilal is preparing the evening meal.

BEA

Mum, you lost it.

Julia stands in the doorway with a perplexed expression, watching the fringed end of the turban cloth pass between her feet.

JULIA

Lucy, have you found the big towel? It was on the railing. I'm sure it was.

Bea makes a revolution of the turban and half-covers one of Lucy's eyes.

LUCY

Bilal is going to sing us a song.

BILAL

Am I?

LUCY

But you have to do it the English way.

Bilal looks at Julia, who smiles and takes an interest.

JULIA

Actually, you have to go into a wardrobe.

Bilal looks at the big wardrobe in the corner of the room.

LUCY

You have to go into the wardrobe and then you can't stop
singing till we tell you.

Bilal seems to think this over.

BILAL

OK.

*Now he is poised, squatting in the wardrobe, with the door ajar.
He takes a last look at the three of them and closes himself in.*

JULIA

You can start now!

*Bilal begins. It is sad, lilting warble of an Arab song, with bright
highlights and a mumbled refrain. Julia rises and passes their shoes
to Bea. With hand over Lucy's mouth and bursting with repressed
laughter, she and both girls sneak out of the door.*

*Now we see just the room and its effects – the discarded sewing,
the tilly lamp, a schoolbook – and the wardrobe singing to itself.*

INT. COURTYARD. NIGHT

*The inside of a none too splendid courtyard in the Medina.
Evening. The light from the little oil wicks mingles with sparse
electric lamps. A kind of concert is in progress. The audience, a
motley assortment of travellers and locals, sit around the group of
singers. The air is filled with the rhythmic, urgent clattering of
metal castanets.*

40

We see the singers – half a dozen men in skullcaps and ceremonial blue robes – seated cross-legged against the wall. These are the Gnaouia. At their centre, a single man plays a primitive bass instrument which emits a hypnotic, liquid counterpoint. We recognize him as Adil. Between the singers and the audience, clay urns emit a belching cloud of incense.

Julia is cross-legged at the front, the girls behind. Next to her is the young, Nordic-blonde woman, Eva, and she is already well transported by the music. Bilal stands to the side of the musicians, clapping, smiling from ear to ear, equally gone.

Gradually, jerkily, Eva gets to her feet, spasmodically moving to the rhythm.

Now Eva is jerking and dancing as if she might tear her frail body apart. A Gnaouia rises from his position and wafts gust after gust of heavy incense into her face. She falls into a crouch, and the Gnaouia gently lays her, twitching and muttering, on to a low couch.

The music regains in intensity. Julia leaps to her feet and there is a fire in her eyes. The girls watch in horror as she moves off towards the musicians.

EXT. HOTEL BALCONY/COURTYARD. DAY

Julia comes on to the hotel balcony. Bea is winding a turban on to Lucy's head.

> JULIA
>
> Bea, you haven't been making Lucy promise things again, have you?

> BEA
> (*through teeth*)
>
> Like?

> JULIA
>
> Like promising not to speak to her mother?

Bea carries on winding the cloth.

You know, it's quite common for daughters to be embarrassed by their mothers.

The turban grows bigger and bigger.

I mean, I remember mine. She even used to put on lipstick, you know, on the top floor of the bus . . .

With the cloth's end in her teeth, and with an esoteric nip and tuck, Bea quietly finishes her masterpiece.

LUCY
Mum, Bea has to say something.

BEA
I have to go to school.

JULIA
Darling, you don't have to do anything . . .

BEA
No. I have to go to school.

JULIA
Well, you can then.

BEA
No, I can't. I need a satchel, which I don't have. I need a white shirt, which I don't have. I need a white skirt, which I don't have.

She stands in the centre of the room, victorious.

So I can't, see.

JULIA
We can go to the bank tomorrow and if the cheque has come from your father . . .

BEA
And what if it hasn't?

42

JULIA

Then we'll go the next day.

BEA

And what if it still hasn't?

JULIA

Then we'll think of something.

BEA

Well, it won't arrive.

JULIA

No, darling . . .

BEA

It won't.

Her face creases up and sudden tears pour down her cheeks.

Because he's forgotten about us.

She goes to the wall again and gives it a vicious, noisy kick.

INT. HOTEL. EVENING

Lucy and Bea are up on the balcony. They watch as Bilal and Julia cross the courtyard. Julia calls up.

JULIA

We have a job! For a Berber poet! I'm a translator!

EXT. HOTEL COURTYARD/BALCONY. NIGHT

Night now. The girls are asleep. Julia is one-fingering the typewriter. Bilal sits against the wall, legs outstretched, smoking a cigarette, his mind elsewhere. Julia pauses at a word in the manuscript.

JULIA

Oh. This word's in Berber, I think.

43

Bilal looks up.

JULIA

Msrot?

He thinks about it.

BILAL

Msrot . . . No. It is impossible. Not in English. Not even in French.

JULIA

Go on. Try.

He thinks about it.

BILAL

Like a great river. No. A boat. Two boats. Yes, two homeless boats.

JULIA
(smiles)

Two homeless boats?

BILAL

Two homeless boats . . .

Their eyes meet and they burst into laughter.

INT. CITY SQUARE. DAY

Late afternoon. A quiet table on a pavement, just beyond the square. The usual hubbub is audible, but distantly. Julia is seated there, with Lucy and Bea on one side; on the other is a French woman in a dark suit, her blonde hair cut in a severe bob. Next to her is an Arab man in his sixties. He wears dark glasses and his whole physical demeanour is strikingly still. He is evidently blind. The rest of the group comprises two Moroccan students, one male and one female. The girl is defiantly westernized.

Julia is reading out loud from a slim pile of typewritten pages.

JULIA

'An Arab Peasant Looks at the Moon

Do you know me? Surely not.
Then how have I offended you, that
you'd go a million miles just to plant your flag
on my dreams?
Listen, America!
I, the poet, Ben Abdul Jalil Nor Edeen make the petition.
I know I don't have much say in the matter
But just a word, America – from one man to another.
How I read my soul by the light of her face.
That she's not what she used to be, nor may ever
again so brightly shine, or rise singing that way
through the dark morning, brushing the stars
from her hair.
So you spared no expense, seducer.
But for both our sakes, my enemy, send her
back to me.
And this I plead, in the name of my soul,
in the name of my people, our revolution.
In the name of the moon.'

*The blind man speaks in Arabic to the translator sitting next to
him. She turns to Julia.*

TRANSLATOR

And Ben Abdul Jalil wants to thank you. And . . . maybe have
the typewriter back.

JULIA

Of course . . . but I've only done ten poems.

*The translator speaks in Arabic to the poet again. They have a
conversation before the translator turns again to Julia.*

TRANSLATOR

Yes. Ten poems. He says a life cannot wish for more.

INT. HOTEL ROOM. NIGHT

It is late and Julia enters with Bea asleep on her back. Wearily, she places Bea on top of the mattress. Lucy knuckles her eyes.

LUCY
Mum, what did he mean, only ten poems?

Julia sits against the wall and closes her eyes for a second.

JULIA
I'm afraid that means we're out of work.

INT. BANK. DAY

A kind, dark face topped with a turban looks down at Julia, who is seated on a chair against the wall. She is long-featured and evidently close to tears.

CLERK
You must leave now, madam. The bank is closed.

JULIA
Will you please look again? Just once more.

She glances up at him, imploring and desperate.

There must have been a mistake.

The clerk leans and touches her elbow.

CLERK
There is no money here for you. Tomorrow. Inshallah.

EXT. BUILDING SITE. DAY

Bilal and his workmates are splitting rocks with sledgehammers. The men toil to the rhythm of the labour gang and runnels of black sweat streak down their whitened faces. Suddenly, Bilal's rhythm accelerates furiously, angrily crushing rock to powder. Now he throws the sledgehammer from him and marches off.

INT. HOTEL. DAY

Julia walks briskly along the hotel landing. She is very close to tears. Looking up at the landing above, she briefly notices one of the Henna Ladies who is wearing a red and white turban. There is no doubt about this: it is definitely the missing towel. Julia looks again, but the woman has gone. She stops in her tracks for a second, then continues down the landing and into her room.

EXT. HOTEL COURTYARD/BALCONY. NIGHT

Evening now. Bilal enters the darkened room and lights the tilly lamp. He finds Julia, who has been sitting in the darkness, her forehead on her knees.

BILAL

What is wrong?

She doesn't answer. He carefully puts his hand on her shoulder.

Julia?

Julia raises her head. Her face is strained and her eyes are red.

JULIA

Nothing. We have no money.

BILAL

No money?

JULIA

None. Absolutely none. Not even for the rent.

BILAL

How can that be? How can you have no money?

She faces him, anger in her eyes.

JULIA

Meaning?

48

BILAL

I only mean . . . you are English . . .

JULIA

Just because I am English doesn't mean I am rich.

For whatever reason, Bilal still looks a little stunned.

Do you think I sell dolls for fun?

BILAL

Yes, but that is just money for the pocket, Julia . . . Surely.

JULIA

Many English don't have any money, you know . . . most of them in fact.

This has all been a little fast for Bilal.

BILAL

Pardon?

JULIA

Just because I am English . . .

He can see her fury and throws up his hands in a gesture of appeasement.

BILAL

No problem.

JULIA

That doesn't mean that . . .

BILAL

Pas problème, Julia!

She scrutinizes his face.

JULIA

Really? Then what is the problem, Bilal?

Bilal hangs his head.

BILAL

    I . . . I have left my job.

EXT. STREET. NIGHT

Rain gusts over the street. Julia and the two girls wait in a shuttered doorway. All three are dressed in their heavy burnous cloaks. With their pointed hoods up over their heads, the girls look like a pair of sinister, miniature monks from the Inquisition.

INT. HOTEL ROOM. NIGHT

The room is dark. Lucy is awakened by the sound of the door opening and sees Bilal leaning against the doorway, swaying badly, picked out by the faint landing light. Their eyes meet in the dark, but his are unfocused. He is badly drunk.

Julia gets out of bed and takes his arm. His voice is thick and slurred.

BILAL

    My friend . . .

He collapses face down on the bed.

    Pardonnez-moi . . . Pardonnez-moi . . . My best friend.

He is instantly asleep.

LUCY
(*whispers*)

    Mum, is Bilal all right?

JULIA

He is just unhappy. Go to sleep, darling.

Lucy turns to Bea, who looks sound asleep.

LUCY

    Bea, does Bilal really have forty brothers?

With neither sound nor gesture, Bea turns her back on Lucy.

INT. HOTEL ROOM. NIGHT

Bea stands on a stool. Julia fixes the hem on a roughly cut-out school dress, pins in her mouth. Bilal is seated on a mattress opposite, stitching a navy-coloured overdress. An Arab radio station is on in the next-door room. Bilal hums along. He looks up.

BILAL

Bea, what did you pay for this stuff?

JULIA

The guy wanted ten dirham, but Bea bargained him down, didn't you, darling?

BEA

Rbara dirham . . .

BILAL

Four dirham? Where did you learn how to do that, Bea?

Julia looks at Bea, who stays silent.

JULIA

I don't know. She does all the shopping now. She just learned it.

Bilal goes back to his sewing. Julia speaks quietly to Bea:

My God. A man that sews . . . Look at him . . .

INT. HOTEL. DAY

Julia and Lucy descend the stairs as Bea comes up in her uniform and satchel. In contrast to the other two, who are dressed in kaftans, Bea is the paragon of neatness.

JULIA

So, how was your first day at school?

BEA

Oh, a little girl wet herself.

51

                          JULIA

And?

                          BEA

Well, the teacher took her to the front of the class. Then she
beat her and beat her with a cane till she stopped crying. Then
the cane broke.

Julia's eyes widen.

                          JULIA

My God, Bea, you can't go back there.

                          BEA

Why not? Of course I can.

Bea walks off, stops, turns.

    Only joking!

*She marches confidently up the stairs and disappears round the
corner.*

EXT. HOTEL COURTYARD/BALCONY. DAY

*Julia is out on the communal landing, gathering her dried washing
from the railing. She enters the room, preoccupied, and crouches to
go through a pile of clothing. Lucy and Bea are lying on top of the
mattress, looking at the ceiling.*

                          BEA

When we go home, can we live in a house with a garden?

                          JULIA
                       (*distracted*)

All right.

                          BEA

And rabbits? In a rabbit hutch?

                          JULIA

Yes, all right.

Does that mean all right yes, or all right maybe?

JULIA
That means all right hopefully.

She stands.

Have you seen my pink trousers? Bilal wasn't wearing them this morning . . .

She wrinkles her nose at the very thought of it . . .

Was he?

She moves back out to the landing and follows the railing down to the central courtyard below.

That's strange.

There is the sound of footsteps on the landing above her and she glances up to see the flash of a green kaftan over pink leggings. She stands there, frozen, looking up as – slowly – the penny drops. Now her eyes are ablaze with anger, startled and cold. She speaks under her breath:

How can they do that?

She starts off across the landing, but Lucy has sensed trouble and jumps behind her.

And we have nothing! Nothing!

Lucy catches hold of the back of Julia's skirt.

LUCY
Mum! Stop! Stop!

But Julia is oblivious. Lucy trips and falls on the landing. The knee of her trousers is torn and she lies there, cradling her leg, as the first tears are squeezed out.

Now she can hear Julia on the upstairs landing, hammering on the door.

Give them back!

A number of doors seem to open simultaneously and Julia's voice is answered by voices in ferocious Arabic. Lucy picks herself up and runs up the stairs.

On the upper landing the two Henna Ladies are confronting Julia, words flying thick and unintelligible. A neighbour has emerged behind them and is pelting Julia with anything she can lay her hands on: a cushion, a slipper, an orange. A flower pot crashes dangerously against the wall next to her.

Julia stoops to pick up the orange and throws it back with ferocious strength at one of the Henna Ladies. It is a good shot and the orange smashes on to the woman's forehead. Briefly, a shocked silence falls; juice and orange pulp trickle down the woman's nose as she stares at Julia with stunned wide, kohl-blacked eyes.

Lucy is pressed against the wall as, with a terrible war-cry, the Henna Ladies rush at Julia, who makes a dash for the exit. Howls and oaths are hurled down the stairs, only to be sent rushing back up. Now the Henna Ladies dash past in screaming retreat, with Julia behind them holding a heavy clay oven above her head. Bea is there as well, standing at the rear of Julia in her school uniform and shouting in hoarse Arabic. Other doors have opened now and other voices are added to the fracas.

Summoning all her strength, Julia heaves the oven in the direction of the two women. It cracks and rattles down the landing, flying into pulverized pieces. Julia moves back a couple of steps, almost on to Lucy's face. All Lucy can seem to notice is the deep gash on the palm of her mother's hand. A trickle of blood runs down her index finger and lands with a first splosh on the tiled floor.

It is more than Lucy can stand. As the row resumes, she flees the scene – down the stairs, along the two-cornered landing.

INT. HOTEL ROOM. DAY

Inside the room, the fight can still be heard. From the landing upstairs, a terrible female scream is matched only by Lucy's as she throws herself on the bed, burying her face in the pillow.

Fade to black.

INT. HOTEL ROOM. EVENING

Bilal is crouching on the mattress next to Julia. She winces as he removes her hand from the basin and cleans the wound.

Now he starts to bandage her. Julia still seems upset and Bilal is tender and patient. Lucy leans next to him. Bea is on the mattress, opposite the three of them, reading.

> BILAL
> And what did you learn today, Bea?

> BEA
> *Aleph, sba, tha* . . .

> BILAL
> And the five pillars of Islam?

> BEA
> Prayer, study, pilgrimage, fasting and charity.

> BILAL
> You really are the little Arab girl . . .

Bilal and Julia glance at each other.

> Bea, wouldn't the schoolgirl like a vacancy?

Bea frowns at him.

> JULIA
> Bilal means a holiday.

> BEA
> But why? I'll fall behind. I just started.

                              BILAL
Just for a while. To get away.

                              JULIA
Will you think about it?

                              LUCY
In Bilal's village!

*Bea's eyes dart to Lucy: so she is in on it too. Bea looks hard at her
open book*

                              BEA
I'll think about it.

INT. BUS. DAY

*The bus hurtles through an empty landscape as Lucy and Bilal sit
together. Julia dozes. Bea watches the passing countryside, eyes
alert.*

*Bilal has taken Lucy's trousers on to his lap and, with needle and
coloured thread, begins to put a patch over where they are torn at
the knee.*

*Now Bea snoozes, only to be woken by a blaring horn as a truck
overtakes the bus.*

*Village after village passes by; then fields blue and red with
cornflowers and poppies; children with sticks in their hands and
flocks of sheep and high-necked camels. The great range of the
snow-topped Atlas mountains is in the background.*

*Bea and Lucy watch as Bilal begins to embroider the patch in
earnest: a tiny bird has emerged and the outline of a flower.*

*They wind past a towering asphalt factory on a hill, light grey on
deep grey, a kind of belching medieval fastness full of crenellations
and cut dirt.*

Now Lucy snoozes and Bea watches impassively as Bilal puts the final touch to the patch. He holds it up, smiling, to Bea: a hibiscus flower and a tiny jewel of a hummingbird, its beak sipping nectar. Gently shaking Lucy from her sleep, he proudly shows it to her.

BILAL

Look . . .

Bleary at first, she regards the little masterpiece.

For you . . .

Bea looks on as Lucy beams with delight.

Finally, they reach a crossroads and the bus comes to a stop.

EXT. VILLAGE. DAY

The four of then pass down a track and into Bilal's village. The village itself is little more than a few dozen squat, whitewashed houses, dilapidated, mean and dusty.

They walk down the track. Julia is hand in hand with the girls, Bilal slightly to the front. The entire village has turned out and now forms something of a procession. A young woman emerges from the crowd and showers Julia with a handful of petals. Bilal turns to Julia, beaming.

BILAL

You see! These are my people!

And then before him is another slightly built young woman. He stops in his tracks.

Fatimah.

She looks back at him. He speaks in Berber.

Why aren't you in Mouley Brahim?

FATIMAH
(*in Berber*)
There is a drought, Bilal, if you don't know. And the crop has
failed. Again.

Julia turns to Bilal, concern in her eyes.

JULIA
Bilal, what's wrong?

BILAL
Everything is fine.

*They watch as a small boy trundles a bicycle which is much too
large for him into the scene and stands there, watching
dispassionately. The bike is a universal rust-brown, with neither
brakes nor tyres.*

JULIA
My God, these people really do have nothing . . .

EXT. VILLAGE. DAY

*The village women have gathered into a small crowd and move
across a courtyard towards a small, windowless house with only a
low opening for a door. One by one, they stoop and enter. Julia
and Bea accompany them. Julia literally has to drag Lucy behind
her. Lucy looks back at a group of men seated on a distant stone
wall.*

LUCY
I want Bilal!

She breaks free from Julia, running towards the group.

LUCY
Bilal!

JULIA
Lucy!

Pas problème, Julia!

Bea and Julia pass into the darkened house.

EXT. BERBER HOUSE COURTYARD. DAY

The house is composed of one large, bare room and inside the light is muted. This is the moment when the women undo their headscarves. It is a celebration of baptism and the baby is passed from hand to hand. Briefly, a little fearfully, Bea holds the infant and its dark face crinkles in a yawn.

An old woman smiles at Julia – a huge, tired face with deep eyes – and speaks to her in incessant Berber.

JULIA

I'm sorry . . .

But the old woman just continues in a storm of words, her face beaming.

Around the walls the women chatter and relax, uncoiling their hair. A young girl, her forehead marked deep and brown in a complex tattoo, kneels before Bea and inspects her features.

Now a little girl enters with a tall, ragged man and guides him to a footstool. The man sits, placing a stick and an enormous skin tambourine on his lap. Bea approaches and gazes hard into the man's features: his eyes are pearly-opaque, unfocused, seeing nothing. Meanwhile, the slight figure of Fatimah watches Julia intently, then slips out of the room.

The singer stands and the room falls silent. The blind man beats a slow rhythm on the tambourine that grows in tempo and complexity until, all eyes on him, he sings a short trailing phrase. The skin drum takes up the refrain. Again, but louder, he repeats the phrase. Now a group of the women give back the chorus in practised, high-pitched unison. To and fro go verse and answer, gaining in intensity, until the entire room seems to move with it.

The old woman takes centre stage, her eyes bright with excitement.
Undoing her headscarf from her shoulders, she ties it low around
her loins. Now the young girl joins her in the dance and, as if on
cue, the remaining women break into a fierce, trilling ululation.
The space overflows with music and this wild, ear-splitting war-
cry.

Julia and Bea look on in astonishment and admiration.

EXT. VILLAGE. DAY

Down in the courtyard, we still hear the singing from the house.
Bilal and Lucy are alone now, and he kneels beside her. She smiles
at him. Bilal takes a comb from his pocket, runs it through her hair
and then gathers the hair into a ball on the crown of her head.
There is a small and ragged length of brown cloth over one of his
shoulders. Removing it, we see it is a tiny jellaba, which he slips
over Lucy's head. He secures the hood and only her face is visible
now.

> BILAL
Now you are the little English boy.

EXT. BARBER'S SHOP. DAY

In the barber's shop, fifteen old men are seated against the wall.
Lucy goes from chair to chair, and they laugh as she pats their
beards with her tiny hand. Lastly, she comes to one old man who
gravely lifts her by the waist and places her on to his knee. He
addresses Bilal in Berber.

> BILAL
He says when you grow up, you will be a good man. He can
see that.

The old man speaks again in Berber.

He says, how many wives? In your country?

Lucy ponders this question.

Oh, thousands and thousands.

Bilal translates. There is a moment's reflection, then the phrase in Berber goes round the room: 'thousands'. Everyone laughs.

The old man speaks in Berber.

He says, wives take money, plenty of it.

The old man speaks.

And trouble. Every wife adds trouble to trouble.

The old man speaks. The room erupts in laughter, Bilal too.

To add this sum would need the power of a great mathematician.

The old man speaks, Bilal smiling in anticipation.

But life passes. Youth is spent.

The old man speaks. Bilal frowns and will not translate. The old man repeats himself. When Bilal speaks, he is deadpan now, avoiding Lucy's gaze.

That is why to neglect a wife . . .

The old man speaks.

. . . is a crime against God . . .

The old man speaks. Bilal looks at him. The old man repeats himself, grim and emphatic now. Bilal is silent for a while, then, eyes to the floor, almost to himself:

. . . and a mortal sin.

Silence falls on the room and its fifteen faces. At a sound, Bilal looks up. Fatimah is standing there, just outside the doorframe, eyes shining and intense.

EXT. HILLSIDE. DAY

Bilal moves down a dusty slope to where Julia is seated on a blanket, an enormous vista before her. He sits next to her. There is a moment's silence between them.

JULIA

Thanks, Bilal.

BILAL

Why?

JULIA

I don't know. Just – thanks.

Silence. A light breeze stirs the air.

I guess I feel sort of, very at home.

BILAL

On the side of a hill?

JULIA

Yes. On the side of a hill.

They smile.

He kisses her shyly on her lips. She responds passionately. Slowly, the tension mounts, both of them glancing around from time to time, nervous of discovery.

Silence resumes, broken only by the remote, disorderly chime of goat bells from some distant hill. A scarlet sunset. They each draw their knees up to their chins and watch as the landscape tumbles, ridge on mountain ridge, the Marrakech plain like a great, green chequerboard beneath them.

BILAL

To fill the eyes. It is important.

JULIA

For the memory of it.

Yes. For when we go.

She turns to him.

JULIA

What?

Now Bilal's gaze is flinty and remote.

BILAL

Tomorrow morning.

JULIA

Why? This is your village, Bilal. We've just arrived.

BILAL

No. I do not have a village. I do not have a village anywhere.

JULIA

Then where are you from?

BILAL

Nowhere. I am from nowhere.

He is silent, distant.

La honte . . . Le monde est fait de honte.

JULIA

The world is made of shame . . .

He doesn't reply at first, then:

BILAL

Yes . . .

JULIA

Sometimes, Bilal, I think I do not know you.

BILAL

I do not have a home anywhere, Julia.

He looks her full in the face.

Tomorrow morning, Julia.

EXT. MOUNTAINSIDE. DAY

A farm truck trundles and bumps along a rough track in a chill mountain dawn. In the back of the truck – a press of strung chickens and mangy goats – crouch Julia, Bilal and the two girls, their burnouses up, huddled against the cold.

EXT. ROAD. DAY

The truck is stopped now and a few cars are parked in front of it. Beyond that is a police car and an army truck. It is a police checkpoint. A uniformed policeman approaches them.

> POLICEMAN
>
> Papiers!

Behind him is a rather nervous-looking, uniformed young country boy with a machine gun over his shoulder – albeit pointed at the ground.

> Papiers!

Julia extends her passport. He scrutinizes them with a kind of routine inspection, matching faces to photographs, then speaks to her.

> And this is your husband?

> BILAL
>
> Yes. She is my wife.

Now wearing her newly patched trousers, Lucy watches him with pleasure and surprise.

The policeman closes the passport and returns Bilal's ID card. But he looks at Bilal, his eyes narrowed.

> POLICEMAN
>
> Don't I know your face?

> BILAL
>
> I don't think so.

The policeman looks at him, long and hard.

POLICEMAN

Maybe not.

He moves on down the road.

EXT. LAKE. DAY

Late afternoon now, the sky full of russet hues and a makeshift camp of blankets strung from trees. Julia is the first to wake. Groggily, she mounts the depression, then stops and gasps, her eyes wide. Before her lies a vast lake, its surface like a great, flat sheet of chrome, a blue haze of hills beyond. Now Lucy stirs and wakes. She shakes Bea.

LUCY

Bea?

Bea opens her eyes.

Where's Mum?

She turns to Bilal, who wakes and raises himself on one arm. A distant voice calls out.

JULIA

Hideous Kinky!

Bilal springs to his feet, laughing and tearing his clothes off as he runs to the shore. With a great splash, he is in, ploughing a white course towards Julia. The girls follow to the water's edge.

Come on in!

They hesitate, watching the adults on the lake.

BEA

Mum's going to become a Sufi, you know.

LUCY

And what do Sufis do?

Bella Riza, Bella Freud, Kate Winslet, Carrie Mullan, Esther Freud

BEA

Sufis live in a mosque and pray all day and never go out.

LUCY

Well, she can't, because she's married to Bilal now.

BEA

Oh, Lucy. Mum's married to Dad. You just don't remember, that's all.

Bea looks off sadly into the distance.

Julia goes crashing out towards the middle of the lake and Balil has to spring to catch up with her. Neck and neck, they change into a breaststroke.

BILAL

Julia, what are you doing?

JULIA

I could swim and swim . . . Maybe I could reach the other side.

They tread water now, breathless. Bilal eyes the distance – possibly miles – to the far shore of the lake.

BILAL

Until you drown, you mean.

JULIA

Fine. I don't know. It just doesn't scare me any more. The annihilation of the ego.

Bilal frowns. Julia clears her face with a handful of water.

You know – the death of the body.

Treading water, he watches Julia's face and sees the two girls – a couple of dark specks on the distant shore.

BILAL

How can you talk like that?

69

He briefly submerges himself and reappears.

> JULIA

Bilal?

> BILAL

How can you people talk like that?

With a rush of white water, he swims off in a fierce overarm. Julia hovers in the lake alone.

EXT. CAMP. NIGHT

It is nearly dark. Bilal sits cross-legged, blowing into the fire. Between puffs, his face emerges, slightly blackened. Lucy sits opposite him.

Julia looks up from the cooking pot and empties the remains of a bag of lentils. She holds it up.

> JULIA

That's the last of it.

> BILAL

God will provide.

> JULIA

Well, I suppose someone has to.

Bilal's face falls, stung.

But Lucy scrambles over and puts her head in his lap. For a time, she watches his stern expression. Very slowly, he softens, then smiles and tousles her hair.

Out of the darkness a bird cries, distant and full of ancient pain.

> LUCY

Is something out there?

> BILAL

No, Lucy. Just everything we could possibly need.

His eyes relax into the darkness.

Everything in the world . . .

EXT. LAKE. DAY

*Lucy and Bea walk towards the shore. The water is mirror-like
and still, and the high, hazy mountains seem to float on the distant
horizon. A thrown stone arcs and plunges beneath the lake's
surface. The girls watch quietly as the ripple blossoms and spreads,
massive, across the water.*

*A far-off, mechanical churning breaks the silence. The girls look
over and their jaws drop. Now round a point of land comes a kind
of pedal boat. It is just near enough for the girls to distinguish a
man at the controls, a figure in a pink bikini next to him. Buoyed
up on the water with its four vast red spheres, its flags and
pennants, it looks not so much a leisure craft as the wild caprice of
a mad sultan. The boat comes to a halt, then, with a sound of
pedals, turns on itself and disappears – a vision – from where it
came.*

The girls scramble down to the shore and find Bilal sitting there.

                    BILAL
It is from the hotel.

                 BEA and LUCY
The hotel?

                     BEA
Have you been there?

                    BILAL
I had a job. With horses.

                     BEA
Can we go there for a ride?

                    BILAL
No. It is nothing. Useless. Plastic.

LUCY

Please?

BILAL

No.

He walks away.

It is a bad place.

EXT. LAKE. DAWN

Julia is at the lakeside. She spreads her little rug on the sand and kneels on it. Opening her hands, book-like, to her face, she begins to pray. From a distance, the girls look on.

EXT. CAMP. MORNING

The sun has risen now, but the girls still have a blanket over their knees, and they lean against a tree, bowls in their laps. They seem dustier than before, with deeper tans. In the near background, Julia approaches.

Entering the camp, she points to Lucy's bowl.

JULIA

Eat it up, darling. It's all we have left.

LUCY

Where's Bilal?

JULIA

He's gone to find food. We'll have lunch when he gets back.

BEA

If he comes back.

They look at Bea, startled.

Well. He's gone a bit potty, hasn't he?

72

EXT. LAKE. DAY

Bilal sits high on a bluff, alone, overlooking the lake. Beneath him, five bright-red pedal boats – the nearest within a stone's throw, the furthest just a crimson speck – seem to perform a complex figure-of-eight on the water's surface. The eerie bump and churn of pedals come across the lake at him.

EXT. CAMP. DAY

Late afternoon. The camp is under a fierce heat. A blanket has been draped over a rope and Julia sits reading at the mouth of this makeshift tent, Lucy next to her. Behind them, where it is dark and cool, Bea is asleep.

> LUCY
>
> Mum, will we still have a garden?

Julia is sleepy and distracted, twiddling her hair into a plait.

> JULIA
>
> Mmm.

> LUCY
>
> And mashed potatoes every night?

> JULIA
>
> Mmm.

> LUCY
>
> And will we go to school sometimes?

> JULIA
>
> Mmm.

> LUCY
>
> And will you still want to have two little girls?

Julia puts down her book and looks at Lucy, suddenly troubled.

> JULIA
>
> What? When?

When you become a Sufi?

They both look up and out from the tent.

JULIA

Bilal . . .

Bea scrambles out from the back and looks over Lucy's shoulders.

Bilal approaches with a white sack over his shoulder. He places it on the ground and removes three tins from it. He begins to juggle them. Julia and the girls smile.

BILAL

Sardines . . .

He stops juggling and, in a clatter of metal cylinders, empties the sack on the ground in front of them.

. . . thirty-six tins.

Their faces fall, and stay fallen.

JULIA

Is that it?

Bilal goes into his breastpocket.

BILAL

No. And two cigarettes . . .

He grins at them, not yet recognizing the shock on their faces.

EXT. CAMP. EVENING

Darkness falls now over the camp and thicket. A fire is lit. Lucy and Bea are on their hands and knees at the perimeter of the rugs, violently throwing up. Julia kneels between them with a hand on either shoulder.

JULIA

We have to go back.

BILAL

Yes . . .

EXT. LAKESIDE. MORNING

Bilal walks down the lakeside, the sack of tins over his shoulder.
He finds his spot and rolls up his sleeves.

Arc on silver arc of sardine tins flies through the dawn light,
disappearing beneath the lake.

Now he stands, hand on hips, and watches the water grow tranquil
and flat.

EXT. ROADSIDE. DAY

A dirt road extends to the horizon. On either side no trees or hills,
just an endless stony plain. Bumpily, a car approaches. Bilal rushes
into frame, his arms waving.

EXT. ROAD. DAY

Julia, Lucy and Bea are squatted in a kind of triangle, their kaftans
round their knees, each taking a piss. On the road beyond them,
the battered car comes to a halt.

Bilal approaches, and they pull up their knickers and get to their feet.

BILAL

This man is called Mohamed. He will drive you to Marrakech.

LUCY

Isn't Bilal coming? Aren't you coming, Bilal?

BILAL

No. There is work in Agadir.

The other two steal off towards the car.

LUCY

But aren't you coming with us?

75

That is no longer part of the plan, Lucy.

Bilal looks round at Julia and Bea. Only the car can be seen. He bends his back and throws a perfect somersault. A puff of sand explodes beneath his feet.

Learn and work, Lucy, that is the only secret. We will meet soon. Inshallah.

Hand in hand, they walk towards the car.

They reach the car and Bilal bundles Lucy into the back seat.

BEA

What did he say?

Lucy says nothing. This is her *secret. Julia stands at the car.*

JULIA

Goodbye, Bilal.

He smiles and waves, and makes his way off down the road, his pack on his shoulder. With one hand on the taxi door, Julia watches him go.

Bilal!

She runs to him, and the girls look on as Julia and Bilal stand in the dusty verge, rocking, clasped in each other's arms.

EXT. CAFÉ. DAY

Julia stands in the crowded Medina, her bags around her feet.

With a yell, Lucy and Bea go running through the crowded terrace restaurant.

BEA

Bastard and bum!

They make a break for the street. Just as they do so, an adult hand comes out and catches Lucy by the forearm. She wheels round and faces her captor. Bea sidles up behind.

Seated alone, an adult man of about fifty confronts them. He is dressed in a pale linen jacket and a blue shirt, buttoned at the collar. His hair is dark and neatly cut, though he is mostly bald. A pair of wire-rimmed spectacles surmount his tanned face, as handsome as it is round. When he speaks, his voice is polished and urbane, with a perfect English accent.

SANTONI

And what will I call you? The English girls? Or the Arab girls?

Guiltily, Bea and Lucy look back at him.

SANTONI

No matter. Shall we have tea?

Their eyes on him, the girls seat themselves. Giving a little nod, the man speaks.

Jean Louis Santoni.

The girls turn round to the street.

BEA and LUCY

Mum!

Now tea is poured from a brass teapot at a great height, and Julia is seated with the two girls on either side of her.

Santoni gives out a loud pleasant laugh.

SANTONI

Good God! Yes! I remember your husband. I knew him in the sixties. Quite a dandy. Does he still wear those gold waistcoats?

BEA
(*evasively*)

Probably . . .

SANTONI

And those little tight, black, elegant shoes, much too small for him. With the pointed toes?

78

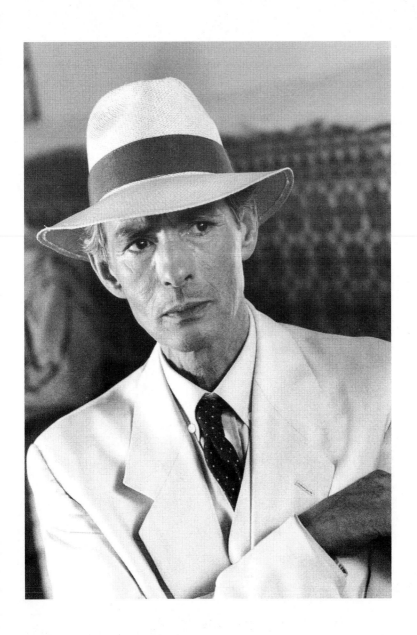

JULIA

I'm sure he does. And despicable red socks. Full of old goat's cheese.

SANTONI

I see . . .

BEA

Do you ever see him?

SANTONI

I'm sorry, Bea. London's such a big place.
(*to Julia*)
Booming actually. Full of raincoats, and pragmatists, optimists . . . bank accounts . . . wives . . .

JULIA

Which is why you're here.

SANTONI

Which is precisely why I'm here. And you?

JULIA

Yes. Something similar.

Santoni gives Julia a hopeless little smile.

SANTONI

I have a house in the Mellah. You must all come and visit.

BEA

Oh, Mum, can we?

JULIA

Of course.

She rises.

But we have to go now.

Santoni rises with them. He opens his wallet.

SANTONI

Here is my card, anyway.

They exit.

EXT. PARK. DAY

*Car horns and traffic sounds. Julia sits on the stairs of a little park.
Lucy is sleeping in her lap, Bea next to her. Lucy stirs and smiles
up at her.*

LUCY

Mum, are you going to write to Bilal?

JULIA

I will, but he'll have to write first, because I don't know where
he is.

LUCY

So he knows where we are then?

JULIA
(*stonily*)

No.

LUCY

But if he doesn't know where we are, and we don't know
where he is . . .

*Lucy's brow knits into a frown: she's trying to think this through.
Julia gazes off levelly into the far distance. She doesn't want to
hear.*

Then he won't be able to write, even if he wanted to.

Silence from Julia.

Would he?

More silence from Julia.

Don't we have an address, Mum?

Julia is stony-faced, then sneezes, then emits a first sob and a tear rolls down her cheek.

Both girls jump to their feet.

Oh, Mum, don't cry.

Which only worsens matters. A flood now, and heaving shoulders.

EXT. VILLA. MAIN DOORS. DAY

An Arab servant pulls at a large wood and metal door and sunlight slices a dusky space. After a momentary exchange, Julia and the two girls enter. Julia talks to the servant as Lucy and Bea stand to the side.

> BEA
> (*whispers*)
> If she asks for money, I'll kill her . . .

The Arab man moves off with Julia's card in hand, leaving the three of them there, their heads craning. In here it is vast and cool – a tiled antechamber of grand proportions. The roof is dominated by a latticed metal lampshade the size and shape of an English postbox, while the fresh whisper of a fountain commingles – somewhere in the shadowy heights – with the sounds of doves.

EXT. VILLA. GARDEN AND FOUNTAIN. DAY

The servant re-enters and beckons them forward. They walk through the garden towards the main house.

INT. VILLA. DAY

The servant ushers them through the door and into the main courtyard. From here, floor upon floor of lacquered banisters climb to a vast open ceiling, magnificently glassed over. There are large Arab couches, paintings, rugs – Jean Louis Santoni's house is little less than a palace. Side-tables are dotted everywhere and every surface is covered with plates and crystal glasses and empty champagne bottles.

In a dressing gown, Santoni enters from a door opposite. Behind him comes a young woman of Julia's age, slim and pretty but with a tired, pinched look on her face. Behind her comes an intellectual-looking man, sour and sick with a hangover.

> SANTONI

I'm afraid you missed quite an average party.

The young woman catches up and stands at his side.

Ah. This is Charlotte. And this is Ben Said.

> CHARLOTTE

Hello. Do excuse the mess.

> SANTONI

Yes. Charlotte won't let the natives within a mile of the glassware, will you, darling?

She exudes a thin smile.

> BEA

Oh, can we help?

> JULIA

I'm not sure if that would be an improvement.

> CHARLOTTE

On the contrary. How sweet!

> BEA

I'm Bea!

INT. VILLA. WEST SIDE CHAMBER. DAY

Now the two girls cross the courtyard, Lucy in front. Each has a tray with a few crystal glasses perched precariously on top.

LUCY
(*whispers*)

Jean Louis Santoni . . .

BEA
(*whispers*)

Hideous Kinky . . .

Approaching the doorway to the rear courtyard, Lucy comes to an abrupt halt. Bea narrowly averts a collision. The crystal rattles and chimes on its tray.

We see what they are seeing – the large table set for breakfast – and in the middle there, enshrined, you would think, in its own shaft of sunlight, a box of cornflakes. The girls devour it with their eyes.

INT. VILLA. WEST SIDE TERRACE. DAY

Now all six of them are seated at the table in the back courtyard. Lucy earnestly munches on her cornflakes.

Bea is on her feet and paces back and forth, a glum expression on her face. Her hands are extended in front of her stomach and seem to suggest that she is cradling an enormous paunch.

JULIA

Santa Claus!

SANTONI

Alfred Hitchcock!

JULIA

Billy Bunter! No! Your father!

Bea stops and looks at Julia.

BEA

No, it's Sheikh Ben Jalil.

JULIA

What?

BEA

That's where Mum's going. Isn't it, Mum?

BEN SAID

The Sufi?

JULIA
(*defensively*)

Yes.

BEN SAID

And you know what to expect of these Sufis?

JULIA

Knowledge, I hope. Some kind of guidance.

BEN SAID

I see. Let me tell you what to expect . . .

He puts his fingers together and glances at her sideways.

To start with, some sitting around on cushions. Actually, much sitting on cushions. A few simple austerities. A great deal of illogic. An even greater deal more incense. Days of fasting. Interminable amounts of prayer. Followed by a personal visit from God – allegedly. It is our country's tragedy, you know. This escapism.

JULIA

I'm not escaping anything. I want to understand the truth.

BEN SAID

And the truth – do you think it will just come and curl on your lap? And purr like a cat? Be warned. They are quite, quite dangerous to the mind, these ancient frauds. They would not be permitted in Europe.

JULIA

Oh no. It's Europe that's been cheated. Of its inner world.

BEN SAID

The world is simply the world, madam. You cannot avoid it.
We must do the best we can.

JULIA

And whose world is that?

BEN SAID

Of present duties. Of passing pleasures.

JULIA

And what's so great about passing pleasures?

He smiles wanly.

BEN SAID

Well, they're certainly more amusing.

JULIA

Oh, sure. Which is fine. You know. You know. Which is fine
for children. Which is fine for kids . . .

The table is a little silenced by her sudden vehemence.

Like cornflakes . . .

SANTONI

Julia, never mind about Ben Said. You see, Ben Said works for
the tax department. Actually, Ben Said *is* the tax department.
And Sufis . . . well, they don't go in for that kind of thing.
(*to Ben Said*)
Do they, my friend?

Julia and Ben Said give out reluctant smiles.

Lucy absent-mindedly claws at her arm.

JULIA

Lucy, don't scratch like that. Show . . .

Lucy presents her arm. There is a small, red rash on the crook of her elbow. Julia reaches deep into the pocket of her kaftan and produces a tin.

I bought this at the Medina.

She struggles with it.

But it won't open.

Lucy extends her hand.

LUCY

Me . . .

Lucy struggles with it, pressing on the tin with the flat of both hands. She passes it to Bea, who wraps it in her shirt, twisting it to no effect. Bea passes it to Charlotte, who takes it and eyes it coldly.

CHARLOTTE

Man's work . . .

She passes it to Ben Said, who merely passes it to Santoni.

Now he struggles with the tin, first tapping it on the table and making a great drama of the thing.

SANTONI

Hmmm . . .

He leans back in his chair, craning round to where the kitchen door lies open.

Abdul-munaim!

A small kitchen boy emerges, dressed in a far-from-white tunic. Santoni addresses him in a mock-stern voice.

Abdul-munaim, I command you to open this tin.

Abdul takes the tin and seems no sooner to touch it than it comes apart in his hands. Julia and Santoni laugh. The boy hands it back with a huge smile.

JULIA

Maybe this will help.

Santoni looks at the contents.

SANTONI

I don't think so, I'm afraid.

He shows a dry, dark wad rattling in the bottom of the tin.

It's boot polish.

CHARLOTTE

Wretched country . . .

But Santoni smiles, and Julia smiles back.

SANTONI

Why don't you stay for a while?
(*to Charlotte*)
You wouldn't mind, would you, darling?

CHARLOTTE
(*eyeing Julia*)

No . . . of course not.

BEA
(*eyes fixed on table*)

Oh, please, Mum.

JULIA

Well – maybe just till we go to Algeria. Until the cheque arrives.

SANTONI

Excellent. You can have your own rooms . . .

JULIA

But just for a day or so.

SANTONI

Of course. And cornflakes and mashed potatoes for my Arab
girls!

Bea and Lucy give back heavenly grins.

INT. VILLA. WEST SIDE CHAMBER. DAY

Morning now. Through the main courtyard and up the staircase, we follow Charlotte as she moves through the villa, a pile of clothes on her arm.

Now she enters a library. A large recessed wardrobe stands before her, its doors ornately gilt in Arab style. Sliding the doors apart, she reveals a veritable wall of men's suits.

As she parts the suits to make a space, Charlotte gasps in fright, revealing the figures of Bea and Lucy in there, peeping up and out, shamefaced, at her.

> CHARLOTTE

Why are you hiding?

> BEA

We're not actually hiding. We're, er . . . sort of exploring.

Charlotte motions them out, and hangs a suit.

> CHARLOTTE

Bea, how long have you been in Morocco?

> BEA

About a year.

Charlotte neatly seats herself on a couch. She pats the space next to her.

> CHARLOTTE

Tell all . . .

INT. VILLA. GARDEN AND FOUNTAIN. DAY

Julia is seated at the big table in the rear courtyard. There is a kind of multiple clacking sound, and Bea and Lucy appear in the doorway, with Charlotte behind them. The first thing we notice is the two girls' faces – their lips smeared in red lipstick, lashes blackened, eyelids daubed in blue eyeshadow. Both pairs of feet are in patent-leather high heels, absurdly big for them. Lucy wears a brocade vest; beneath that, a collarless man's shirt. Bea is in a kind of black cocktail number that reaches to her ankles. On her neck is a set of pearls.

JULIA
(*smiling*)
Good heavens. You look – grotesque.

With a whoop, the girls discard their shoes and go flying off back into the light of the house. Charlotte enters and sits opposite Julia.

BEA
(*off*)
Bugger and bum!

LUCY
(*further off*)
Bastard and bum!

CHARLOTTE
You know, that language is going to land those girls in trouble. Children need discipline, Julia.

JULIA
Do you think so? I had plenty of that in my own childhood. I can't say it did me the slightest good.

CHARLOTTE
No. I could probably say the same. Unfortunately.

With a shout and a slam, the girls re-enter. They settle at the table and watch the adults through their painted faces.

But don't you think it's time you went home?

JULIA
You mean to a one-room flat in south London?

CHARLOTTE

But surely better than here . . .

JULIA

Or home in the evening with the two of them rigid from childminders and television? Or fourteen working hours a day and nothing to show at the end?

CHARLOTTE

Yes, but surely . . .

JULIA

I'm sorry, Charlotte. These are things you just don't know about.

CHARLOTTE

Of course. Children are a gift. But that doesn't give you the right to put them in danger.

JULIA

What?

CHARLOTTE

I mean, Julia, that doesn't give you the right to just drag your children around Morocco . . . in the company of escaped criminals.

JULIA

What? What on earth are you talking about?

Julia's gaze settles on Bea.

Bea?

Bea looks guiltily back.

What have you been saying?

BEA

So why did he lie? So how come the policeman knew his face?

JULIA

Whose face? Bilal?

BEA

So what about Fatimah? What about his wife?

JULIA

Bea, what wife?

BEA

Oh, never mind.

Bea looks away, exasperated.

JULIA

Bea . . .

BEA

So how comes he had to go to Agadir? How come we had to hide at the lake? How come we had to leave Marrakech?

JULIA

Bea, that was just a holiday.

BEA

Yeah – on the *run*.

JULIA

Oh, Bea . . .

LUCY

Mum, does that mean Bilal can't come and stay with us here?

Charlotte's eyes widen and her hand flies to her throat.

CHARLOTTE

Lucy, God forbid . . .

EXT. VILLA. GARDEN. DAY

Julia stops in her tracks at the sight of Bea blindfolded, arms flailing, on the garden path. Charlotte dodges Bea deftly. From a distance, Julia watches as the two laugh together.

INT. VILLA. BEDROOM. EAST SIDE CHAMBER. NIGHT

Distantly, there is a call to prayer. Inside her spacious room, Julia is kneeling on her prayer mat. From somewhere in the house comes a scream, a laugh, the sounds of commotion. She rises and goes to investigate.

INT. VILLA. NIGHT

In the villa the lights have been extinguished. Julia leans over the darkened first-floor banister and down to the courtyard below, where a slide projector throws a luminous white oblong on an opposite wall. Bea stands there in the light, breathless. Santoni mans the tripod. On one side of him Charlotte is seated; her cigarette smoke curls and billows in the beam. On his other side is Abdul-munaim. Lucy sits – feet swinging – in an enormous Berber armchair of the type on which the fate of nations is decided. With a nod, she literally cues Santoni. He puts his hand in front of the projector beam and its silhouette fills the wall.

LUCY

. . . No. It was the Black Hand . . .

Santoni wobbles his hand menacingly, fingers spread. Removing it, Bea is caught again in the full glare of the bulb.

She ran and ran, but she couldn't escape.

Bea dashes back and forth from one end of the shining rectangle to the other, her shadow chasing her.

And no one was waiting at home for her.

Bea throws her hands to her face and rolls her eyes. It's pure Victorian melodrama. Santoni carries a long, thin metal object into the beam and its twin blades darkly chop and gnash at Bea's tiny figure.

Only the Hideous Scissors!

Bea spins on the spot and screams in terror and delight. To Julia, it's obvious that Bea is just a normal, excited little girl here, and happy to be that.

Julia sadly closes her eyes and turns away.

INT. BEDROOM. MORNING

Lucy and Bea go into the bedroom. Bea stops in her tracks. The tartan dufflebag, packed and full, its old notorious self, is draped over the top of the bed.

> BEA
>
> The cheque's arrived.

> LUCY
>
> Bea, you have to tell Mum. You do.

Their eyes fill with alarm as they hear Julia approach. She enters.

> JULIA
>
> The money's come, but not as much as we need. So we're going to hitchhike to Algiers.

She watches the girls' faces for their response.

> LUCY
>
> Mum, Bea has something to say.

Julia sits on the bed.

> BEA
>
> Mum, I've talked to Charlotte. She says I can stay here till you get back.

Julia considers this.

> JULIA
>
> Is that what you want?

BEA
If you really want to go.

JULIA
And what does Charlotte say?

BEA
She says this is no place for little girls to run wild in.

Julia sits on the edge of the bed and seems to stare into space.

I don't need another 'adventure', Mum.

Julia is silent.

I have to go to school. I have to learn things.

Pause.

I'll still be here when you get back.

Pause.

JULIA
Fine.

She slips to the floor and leaves.

BEA
I never thought she'd say that.

They listen to Julia's footsteps recede along the landing.

You know, Lucy, you don't have to go either. Not if you don't want to.

She lies back on the bed and murmurs to herself:

Hideous Kinky . . .

EXT. MEDINA. DAY

Dufflebag in tow, Julia and Lucy move down the narrow laneway and away from the villa.

Bea walks next to them, dressed in her school uniform. At the corner, Julia kneels beside Bea and gives her a hug. Bea smiles at Julia and Lucy, a smile that is at once bright and vague. They watch her go down the street, a satchel over her shoulder. She joins two little Arab girls dressed in identical outfits and they move off together.

> LUCY
> (*quietly*)

See you soon, Bea . . .

EXT. ROAD. DAY

Just beyond the old gates of Marrakech, they find some shade beneath a tree. A single car approaches and accelerates past their outstretched thumbs.

Now on the road – nothing. Just the fierce, mad, scrape-sawing of cicadas. A figure appears in their direction, his thumb out at another car. It doesn't matter as the car passes them all. He joins them in the shade and Lucy takes in this character: a scrawny, dusty young man, his hair at all kinds of angles, a fluffy chin-beard and an improbable pair of trousers that look like he has made them himself. He carries only a small canvas knapsack and settles himself a little apart from them.

> JULIA

Algiers?

He looks at them distractedly and points to himself.

> HENNING

Henning. Henning.

Julia points back.

> JULIA

Henning . . .

HENNING

Algiers.

They sit in silence. Now, in single file, five variously turbaned old men pass side-saddle on emaciated donkeys. Each group looks – incuriously – at the other.

JULIA

Rush hour . . .

Henning smiles and lazily nods, as if he's got the joke, though it's perfectly obvious he hasn't.

With a roar, a very large and battered truck approaches them. Julia jumps to her feet – this looks like serious business.

INT. TRUCK. DAY

Inside the cab, Julia and Lucy sit next to the driver. The man's thick hands grasp the wheel as they speed down the road.

JULIA

Algiers?

He looks her full in the face, his own smeared and ruddy, eyes blackened like a pantomime demon: hair springs, thick and sooty, from every imaginable part of his features. His only answer is to slam the vehicle into top gear. Julia and Lucy are thrown back into their seats.

Lucy watches as they recklessly overtake the group of old men and their donkeys, and Julia's knuckles go white against the dashboard.

Lucy looks back through the rear-view window. On the other side of the glass, Henning's grimy face is pressed close to hers. She smiles faintly; he looks through her.

Further along the road is clear and it hurtles beneath the dashboard like some deadly ticker-tape. A group of camels is overtaken. Lucy looks back and Julia follows her gaze. Henning is asleep in the corner of the truck.

JULIA
He'll get sunstroke.

LUCY
Is it very hideous to . . .

JULIA
Yes. Very.

INT. TRUCK. NIGHT

The truck comes to a halt, waking Julia and Lucy.

The driver leaves the cab, but soon returns, throwing a blanket over himself like a shroud.

JULIA
I think that's us for the night. Funny. It feels like the
mountains. I don't remember any mountains on the map.

EXT. TRUCK. DAWN

From their corner in the back of the truck, Lucy's tousled head appears from the sleeping bag. Henning lies opposite, curled in on himself, only a thin jacket over him.

Careful not to wake Julia, Lucy extricates herself and picks her way to the side of the vehicle. We see she is wearing the Manchester United football shirt. By the light of early dawn, a vast landscape lies beneath her: mountainous and inhuman, deeply clad in brilliant, pink-lit snow. Lucy peers over the side and begins to sing – softly at first, but growing in confidence and volume, till she is chanting at the top of her voice.

LUCY
Hamal – Bi – lal – al – Ham. Albi – lal.

Now there are just the truck – tiny in this snow-filled landscape made for giants – and Lucy's little voice, echoing, rolling from peak to peak, filling the world.

Lal – Hashish – Roofrack – Ramadan – Jellybeans – Jellybal –
Sunstroke – Akabar – Annihilation . . .

From a far distance, an unseen farmdog adds its voice to the event.

EXT. TRUCK. MORNING

*Now the driver is out of the cab and pissing in a field. Julia crosses
the truck and gives Henning a nudge.*

> JULIA
> Henning?

He comes to.

> HENNING
> Algiers?

*He sits upright and Julia removes a bundle of cloth from her
kaftan. Kneeling beside him, she begins to wind a turban on his
head. Lucy comes up from behind.*

> LUCY
> Mum, that's my turban.

> JULIA
> It's just so he won't be so mad, darling. You're got a spare
> one.

*She wets the loose end of the turban with a handful of water and
begins to bathe his blistered face and mouth.*

EXT. ROAD. DAY

Julia and Lucy are seated next to the driver again.

*They're on a mountain road now. A large truck heads towards
them and the driver guns the vehicle with only inches to spare.
There is a deafening exchange of horns. Lucy and Julia look down
as the road beneath vanishes and a gaping chasm opens up. Lucy
looks round again to see Henning facing backwards at the rear of*

the truck. He stands with his arms raised in the posture of crucifixion. A great cloud of dust engulfs him.

Suddenly, a solitary camel appears ahead of them. The driver swerves. The truck veers dangerously off the road and comes to a halt. For a moment, the day's silence settles around them, then, gathering up her bag in one hand and Lucy in the other, Julia opens her door and the two of them jump down from the cabin. Henning watches as they pass the sleepy-looking camel and walk off down the road, which is unvarying, trafficless and desolate.

EXT. ZAOUIA. DAY

The screen is black. Iron gates groan on their hinges as they open on to the Sufi courtyard. Lucy and Julia are led inside by an Arab man. He is heavily built and his head sprouts quills of henna-red hair from every pore of his face. A perfect green of a turban surmounts this arrangement. The man's great eyes bore like hot coals into Julia's face.

Reaching an arched door, the man throws Julia a glance and enters, shutting it behind him.

Julia kneels and removes a handkerchief from her pocket, and Lucy grimaces as Julia wets it with saliva and dabs her face with it.

They walk off down the courtyard.

> MAN
>
> Are you from London?

> JULIA
> (*tiredly*)
>
> Yes.

> MAN
>
> Leicester Square . . .

                              JULIA
                             (*tiredly*)
    Yes.

                              MAN
    East Action . . .

Julia is now too exhausted to reply.

                              MAN
    Yes. Tunnel Street. My cousin lives there. Mounaim Hajjam.
    Do you know him?

                              LUCY
    Is Sheikh Bentounes in there?

Julia bites her lip.

                              JULIA
    Yes, darling.

                              LUCY
    Is he coming out?

                              JULIA
    I don't think so, darling. He's dead.

INT. ZAOUIA. DAY

*Lucy and Julia now stand in the Zaouia courtyard as the funeral
procession emerges with a corpse borne high on a bier and
wrapped in white cloth.*

INT. ZAOUIA. NIGHT

*Their sleeping quarters comprise a tiny, bare room with a single
mattress next to a window that opens on to night.*

                              LUCY
    Mum, how long are we going to stay here?

Julia is occupied with the unpacking.

As long as it takes.

Lucy removes her turban and the top half of her forehead is dyed blue. She smiles up at Julia, who bends and kisses her.

Look at you.

Lucy grins back.

INT. ZAOUIA. DAY

Lucy wakes alone in their bare room. She moves to the window. Her face creases up as, down in the courtyard, she sees a hopscotch grid marked out with chalk and a dark-haired figure seems to dash by, just out of her vision. She leans out further. Nothing.

Coming down from the window, she turns to face the door and jumps in fright. Bea stands there in silence, dressed in her school uniform.

LUCY
Bea . . . How did you get here? Did Charlotte bring you?

BEA
No, I walked, didn't I?

The two girls look at each other.

Because you've forgotten about me, haven't you? Both of you.

LUCY
No, Bea . . .

BEA
And you don't have to worry about Bilal any more.

Lucy's face brightens.

LUCY
Bilal?

                              BEA

    Because I'm his favourite now.

                             LUCY

    Oh, Bea . . .

Bea's face darkens into a frown.

                              BEA

    What the hell is that?

Lucy follows Bea's stare. Looking down at herself, her face explodes with fright. A stump of a hand, dark and heavy, has fixed itself to the front of her nightshirt. Right on cue, it begins to swarm up her chest, making for her throat.

INT. ZAOUIA. DAWN

Julia wakes with a start. Lucy's back is next to her. Her nightshirt is wet and tangled round her waist, and on the mattress where she lies is a huge dark stain of warm urine.

INT. ZAOUIA. DAY

The bedsheet has been washed and hangs in the room to dry. Lucy sits on the bed and watches as Julia brushes her long hair out. Going into her bag, Julia removes a small package of black velvet in which a tiny fragment of broken mirror is wrapped. With the aid of this, she applies lipstick to her mouth and purses her lips, checking her teeth.

                             LUCY

    Mum, where did you get lipstick?

                             JULIA

    I have an appointment. With the new sheikh.

A little boy enters the room.

    One moment.

She kisses Lucy on the forehead, smiles excitedly, rises and leaves.

INT. ZAOUIA. DAY

The little boy leads Julia through a large arched door. In there, the new sheikh, Sheikh Habas, is seated in an enormous armchair. The room is large and cool and radiantly still. The sheikh himself is in his early forties, with a luxuriant dark beard and a great peony rose of a pink turban on his head. A glass of mint tea stands on an inlaid table at his side.

> JULIA
>
> I'm sorry about Sheikh Ben Jalil.

> HABAS
>
> Oh, he was getting very old. And a little unruly.

He smiles.

> Of course, we holy men are not meant to say that kind of thing.

Habas looks at Julia with penetrating self-assurance.

> So. You are from London. Do you have work there?

> JULIA
>
> Well, I have a family . . . Sheikh Habas, I wanted to ask about spiritual *barakha*.

> HABAS
>
> Of course. And your age?

> JULIA
>
> Twenty-five.

> HABAS
>
> And father? And mother?

> JULIA
>
> They are both dead.

HABAS

And children?

JULIA

Yes two.

HABAS

And they are here? With you?

JULIA

One is.

HABAS

I see. Yes, I believe I saw her. Very small. With a big weight on her head. And your husband?

JULIA

Yes, he lives in London.

HABAS

So you are apart?

JULIA

Yes.

HABAS

And you still have feelings of love for this husband?

Julia looks at him and frowns. Then she hangs her head.

JULIA

Actually, he is not my husband. And yes. Yes, I do.

A tear trickles down the bridge of her nose, followed by another.

I'm sorry.

She wipes her face with the back of her hand.

That's a bit of a surprise.

HABAS

No. Tears are for memory. They are a gift from God.

She looks at him.

Without them, how could we remember ourselves, let alone remember Him?

There is a long silence and he watches her with quiet eyes. Then, sudden and noisy, a huge sob seems to leap out of Julia's throat and she catches it with her hand.

JULIA

I'm not ready, am I?

INT. ZAOUIA. DAY

Julia and Lucy remove a bedsheet from a large iron tub and, one at either end, twist it, wringing it out.

LUCY

Mum, is it really my birthday in two weeks?

JULIA

Yes. Two weeks and one day actually.

LUCY

So that means Bea's birthday is in one week and one day.

Julia gives the sheet a final twist and a curtain of water cascades from it.

JULIA

Yes. Shall we give her a party?

Lucy's eyes widen.

LUCY

Yes, please.

EXT. MARRAKECH. DAY

Outside Jean Louis Santoni's villa, Lucy and Julia are hammering on the big wood and metal doors. The house is shuttered and dark; only silence comes from within.

111

*Then, tentatively, Ben Said's face appears round the door. He is
bleary-eyed and tired, and he wears a crumpled Egyptian dressing
gown. Julia breaks into a big smile.*

JULIA

Hi!

BEN SAID

Oh . . .

JULIA
(her face drops)
What? Is something wrong?

BEN SAID

Your daughter is not here, I'm afraid.

JULIA

What?

BEN SAID

This is my home, you see, and – well, I had to ask them to
leave.

JULIA

Your home? So? Where did they take her?

BED SAID

Well, they didn't.

JULIA

Ben Said . . . where is my daughter?

BEN SAID

They moved up north. Bea just wouldn't go. I think she was
afraid of losing touch with you.

Julia stares blankly at him.

Actually, it was *quite* a scene. Terrible, in fact.

JULIA

And where is she now?

BEN SAID

Then she wasn't very fond of me, you know . . .

JULIA

And?

BEN SAID

And she went to the big commune, I think.

JULIA

You think?

BEN SAID

Madam . . .

JULIA

Oh, my God . . .

BEN SAID

. . . Everything will be fine.

JULIA

Oh, my God . . .

She covers her face with her hands.

I have lost my daughter.

EXT. MARRAKECH. NIGHT

Lucy stands apart on the pavement, groggy, dressed in her hooded burnous. Julia is at the door of a tall, benighted building. Again and again, she hammers at it, frantic. There is no response, only the distant barking of dogs. Then, from the topmost window, a shutter is opened and a face appears. Julia stirs and shouts up.

JULIA

Where's Eva?

GREG

Eva, oh, she's in the desert. God's there . . . you know . . .

JULIA

Is my daughter here?

GREG

OK. You're Bea's old lady. Hold on.

He closes the shutters.

He reappears at the ground-level door, wrapped now in a woman's floral dressing gown. We remember him as the hippy from before.

JULIA

So she's staying here.

GREG

Sure. Then she went to score cigarettes and . . .

JULIA

Cigarettes?

GREG

I mean, if Bea needs to go and live in a polio orphanage.

JULIA

Polio?

GREG

With 'Patricia' . . .

JULIA

Patricia? Patricia who?

GREG

You know, some Christian fanatic bitch, man.

JULIA

Then where does she live?

GREG

Search me, lady . . . She just turned up.

JULIA

Well, what does she do?

GREG

I don't know. Sort of con-vert people, I guess.

JULIA

Con-vert?

GREG

Hey, don't worry about Bea, lady. I told her, say 'shithouse'.
It's a 'shithouse'. But would she say that? I mean, what's a
'toilet', man! That kid. She's trouble. Truly.

*Without a word, Julia leaves him with a savage stare. Taking
Lucy's hand, she marches off down the street.*

EXT. BUILDING SITE. NIGHT

*The sounds and noise of the quarry at night. A human chain
carries lime sacks, their upper bodies a ghostly, powdered white
against the tungsten arc-lights. When Julia addresses them, their
eyes are pink, their teeth yellow.*

JULIA

Où est Bilal? Où est Rashid? Vous connaissez?!

The men laugh.

EXT. SQUARE. DAY

*Very early morning. Lucy and Julia sit out at the café table, the
square before them. Their faces are tired and strained. Julia
suddenly sees a solitary figure. This is twelve-year-old Aziz, Bilal's
assistant from the Hadaoui scene. She jumps to her feet.*

JULIA

Aziz!

She goes to run after the figure, but first turns to Lucy.

Don't move, all right?

(*off*)

Aziz!

Lucy nods.

All right? You're *glued* to the chair.

Lucy nods.

All right?

Julia dashes off into the square, but immediately reappears. Grabbing Lucy by the wrist, she yanks her from her seat.

INT. ORPHANAGE. DAY

Julia and Lucy are in the whitewashed hallway of an institution. Aziz passes out of the main entrance and leaves them. At the far end comes the sound of a children's party. They stand there, and their faces conceal their horror as a small boy with twisted legs claws himself, belly-down, along the floor towards them. He wears a kind of white smock, his head is shaven and he is smiling at them.

Now a European woman appears at the end of the hall. There is the sound of sensible shoes and she moves briskly towards the small boy, sweeping him up in one arm. He hangs there, still smiling, his legs writhing slightly.

The woman looks at Julia and Lucy. She is in her mid-thirties, smart and prim, a kind of stubborn plainness on her face. This is Patricia.

PATRICIA
You must be Julia. Please wait there.

Patricia exits. The swing doors move behind her.

117

INT. ORPHANAGE. DAY

They enter a large, featureless dining area where a trestle table is erected, with perhaps a dozen boys on either side. All of their heads are shaven, and crutches and walking sticks lean beside them. Pools of lemonade and leftovers are strewn across the table. Julia and Lucy move into the room and all eyes follow them. Patricia places the small boy on a chair.

> PATRICIA
>
> So, you made it. Just in time actually.

Bea is seated at the head of the table. Seeing her sister and mother arrive, she gets up and approaches them with a plate of sponge cake in either hand. She looks quite transformed. Her hair is braided in a tight, Germanic plait and she wears a red and white checked gingham dress, complete with puffed short sleeves and a white laced bib.

> BEA
> *(to Lucy)*
> Would you like some of my birthday cake?

Lucy takes the plate, avidly stuffing the cake into her mouth. Julia moves towards Bea with outstretched arms.

> JULIA
> Happy birthday, darling.

Bea shrinks back and places herself behind Patricia.

> LUCY
> It's my birthday soon.

Patricia looks down at Lucy with cold indifference.

> PATRICIA
> Really?

> JULIA
> I brought you a present, darling.

Julia extends a small red and white necklace. Seeing it, Bea re-emerges from behind Patricia. She turns her back on Julia and with both hands raises her hair from the nape of her neck. Julia fastens the necklace.

Patricia puts a hand on Bea's shoulder.

> PATRICIA
> You've never had a party like this before, have you, dear?

> BEA
> Never.

Bea remains with her back turned to everyone.

> PATRICIA
> You know, Lucy and Julia have nowhere to stay tonight. Shall we make up a bed for them?

> BEA
> Maybe.

Julia watches the back of Bea's head, pained.

> PATRICIA
> Then we can all sit down and have a nice talk about our Lord Jesus.

Now everyone looks at the back of Bea's head.

> BEA
> Maybe.

A flicker of surprise crosses Patricia's face.

EXT. ORPHANAGE ROOF. DAY

Lucy and Bea are out in the courtyard, seated alone at the top of the steps. Down below, a boy pulls himself on crutches across the paving stones, his feet dragging behind him.

LUCY

Is Patricia your mum now?

Bea crouches and loosens a large piece of concrete from the top of the steps.

Mum won't like that.

BEA

Really?

Heaving it into the courtyard below, it smashes into powder and chunks.

INT. ORPHANAGE. NIGHT

In a small black room, Julia and Lucy are cramped together on a single wire-sprung bed. A candle stub lights the space.

LUCY

Mum, why does Patricia hate me?

JULIA

I don't know, darling. She certainly detests your old mum.

She sighs.

Well, I suppose it's what Bea always wanted.

LUCY

To be an orphan?

JULIA

No, darling. To be normal.

EXT. ORPHANAGE COURTYARD. DAY

Dressed in the same Sarah Lee-cake, puffed-sleeve dress, a bow in her hair, Bea moves from one shaved head to another, serving the boys with plates of breakfast bread.

Finally, she joins the end of the table where Julia and Lucy are seated. A large cup of coffee has been set before her. Bea takes a sip from it and drops fall down the front of her dress in a brown stain. Patricia leans forward.

PATRICIA

Coffee . . . Honestly, Julia, just because the child wants coffee doesn't mean she should have it.

She dabs at the stain.

It's ridiculous.

She ruffles Bea's hair.

My poor little orphan.

Julia's eyes blaze and she smashes her plate on the table, silencing the room. Patricia stands.

I insist we go next door. If you have to argue.

JULIA

I insist I'll do as I please.

PATRICIA

Of course. Have you ever done differently?

BEA

Don't, Mum, because . . .

JULIA

No, Bea. I'm your mother. Not her.

Patricia goes and opens the door, standing in the doorway. Julia brushes past her and the door closes behind them.

The two girls stand facing the door. Raised voices can be heard.

LUCY

What are they saying?

Bea sneaks over and puts her ear to the door. She listens, then moves back in close to Lucy and whispers in a cupped hand.

Kinky . . .

Now Bea dances off, skipping and jumping, hopscotch-style, round and round the big table. One by one, stick, spoon and crutch, the crippled boys begin to hammer out their own wild rhythm on the tabletop.

Lucy stands there watching as the volume grows riotous and the air fills with revolt. Bea moves in circles, arms crossed and feet flying, absorbed in her solitary mad sailor's hornpipe.

EXT. HOTEL COURTYARD. DAY

It's morning again in the Hotel Mouley. Landing by landing, there is the to and fro of residents, doors closing, the sounds of radios.

Julia and Bea are back in the toilet queue on the stairs, while on the landing above one of the Henna Ladies has noticed them and leans from the railing, waving brightly. She is also dressed in Julia's pink trousers.

HENNA LADY
Bonjour, mes amies!

She turns to her door.

Miriem!

The other Henna Lady appears in her purple kaftan. He long hair is down, glistening with palm oil.

MIRIEM
Bonjour, mes amies!

Julia and Bea look back and up, smiling warily.

INT. HOTEL. DAY

Only Lucy remains in the hotel room, asleep on her mattress. She stirs and sees a mysterious figure standing in the doorway, framed

*against the light. Detail by detail, she takes in this vision: a
sumptuous globe of a turban fastened with an enormous jewel; a
green and gold brocade frock-coat; a broad embroidered belt
which secures a flintlock pistol; a gemmed powder case; a curved
scimitar and sheath; a pair of baggy trousers disappearing at the
calf into tooled leather riding boots with spurs, and toes like curly
dog's ears.*

*Only now does Lucy take in the face behind the spectacle. Clean-
shaven, dark and beaming brilliantly, it is Bilal.*

*Lucy flies out from under the sheets and he leans towards her. She
throws her arms around his neck and they spin around the room.*

LUCY

Bilal! Bilal!

*He sets her down and straightens his turban. Lucy stands there,
watching him admiringly.*

BILAL

What do you think? I have a job. For tourists. And a horse.
Called Magnificent.

They stand there, smiling at each other.

Look . . .

*His hand goes to the hilt of his scimitar and begins to draw it from
the sheath. A sound from the doorway makes them both look
around.*

*It is Bea, standing there with a towel over her arm. All she sees is
the glittering, half-sheathed blade, then the familiar features of
Bilal. Throwing her hands to her head, she gives out an ear-
piercing scream.*

EXT. RESTAURANT. DAY

*The four of them are seated at an outdoor restaurant by the city
square. Bilal is dressed in a cheesecloth shirt. Lucy sits beside him,*

wearing his big embroidered belt. Bea is on the far side of Julia, eyeing the proceedings darkly.

Lucy fingers the belt and squints up at Bilal with that very special smile. It's clear what is on her mind.

> BILAL

No, Lucy. It belongs to the boss. And, you know, if the boss gets angry . . .

> LUCY

Does the boss pay you himself?

> BILAL

Yes. And overtime . . . and bonuses for special days!

Both the adults laugh. A waiter arrives with menus.

Anything you want. Anything at all.

> LUCY

Does that mean Bilal can take us back to London?

> JULIA

No, darling. That means you can have a Fanta.

> BILAL

And later we will take a carriage to Khatoubia tower. Then to the Menara lake.

> JULIA

Bilal, I don't think so . . .

> BILAL

No. Tonight, I insist.

He spreads his arms, beaming with pleasure.

Marrakech is ours.

Bea suddenly rises from her seat. Her fingers go to her throat and her hand covers her eyes. She seems to sway slightly.

Bea.

With a crash of cutlery and plates, Bea falls to the pavement.

> JULIA

Bea!

INT. HOTEL. NIGHT

In the hotel room, Bilal gently lays Bea out on the mattress. Behind him stands a portly Arab man in a suit. Beyond that is just the sound of Lucy crying inconsolably.

> JULIA
> (*gently, off*)

Shhh, Lucy.

EXT. HOTEL COURTYARD/BALCONY. NIGHT

Julia is out on the landing, elbows on the railing, her face in her hands. The doctor comes out of the room.

> JULIA

It isn't polio, doctor, is it?

> DOCTOR

No, it's streptococcus. And just as dangerous.

He takes out a pad and detaches a page.

Here is the medication. I will come tomorrow.

Julia takes the page and reads it.

Can you afford this, madam?

She looks at him, fear in her eyes.

> JULIA

It's so expensive . . .

> DOCTOR

Yes. I'm afraid your western companies are not kind to we Africans.

He picks up his bag and makes to go.

I suggest you find some way of taking these children home. Don't you agree?

JULIA

I suppose so.

Julia and Bilal look at one another for a long moment.

LUCY

Will Bea die now, Bilal?

She looks up at him with her red eyes.

BILAL

Lucy, Bea would never do anything she didn't want to do.

INT. HOTEL. DAY

Bea is sitting up in bed now, a scarf around her neck. Her face is pale and there are dark circles under her eyes. She raises a metal tumbler to her lips and swallows with a grimace.

LUCY

Does it hurt?

Bea glares at her and her voice is a rasping whisper.

BEA

Of course it hurts.

She puts the cup down.

Tell me a story.

LUCY

Have I told you about the story of the black hand?

BEA

About 122 times, yes.

Lucy hovers there, unsure of the meaning of that.

So go on.

Bea snuggles down beneath the covers.

LUCY

Well. The nice black hand was nice. Especially to little girls . . .

EXT. MARRAKECH. DAY

Very early morning and the long straight road outside the hotel is deserted. In the still air, only the languid clip of hoofs on cobblestones announces the approach of twenty horsemen in full Berber regalia. The procession moves in a slow single file, the men on their powerful white mounts with their muskets up at an angle. Slow as they are, a little figure on the pavement has to struggle to keep abreast of them, now rushing forwards, now running backwards, with her features to the sky.

From his saddle, Bilal looks down at Lucy with a mixture of affection and embarrassment. Mounted on the horse behind, a face black as coal grins from ear to ear.

LUCY

Bilal?

He cocks an eyebrow: what?

Bilal?

Lucy stops and the procession moves on. Just for a moment, Bilal looks over his shoulder at her diminishing figure. The last horse passes and Lucy stands alone in the deserted street, watching them trail off into the distance.

Bilal.

Her chin quivers and her face creases up.

It's Bea . . .

She bursts into tears.

INT. HOTEL. DAY

On the landing, there is a small commotion: the sound of footsteps running, a door slammed. Briefly Julia appears at the doorway to her room. She is dishevelled and wide-eyed.

JULIA

Where's the doctor! Where's the fucking doctor!

She rushes back to the room and cradles Bea in her arms.

Bea!

Bea's head lolls on Julia's elbow. Her face is blue; her lips are almost black. An Arab woman enters the room.

WOMAN
(*in French*)

Her tongue! Find her tongue!

Julia stickily parts Bea's lips and puts her finger in her mouth. A short, rasping sound comes from Bea's throat. A woman's voice comes from the landing.

WOMAN'S VOICE
(*in French*)

He's here! You – get your fat arse up here right now!

EXT. HOTEL COURTYARD. NIGHT

It is evening now and Bilal enters the hotel, carrying his uniform and sword in a large canvas holdall. He passes along the landing and fright crosses his eyes as – from a half-opened door, or the upper railing, or the open stairwell – all faces silently watch him.

INT. HOTEL. NIGHT

Bilal enters the room. Julia and Lucy are crouched on either side of the mattress. Bea lies between them, her limbs drawn straight and her face unmoving, drained of colour. The bedsheet has been pulled up to her neck and looks unnaturally smooth and flat. On

the low table next to them is an assortment of lotions and pills.

Julia looks up at Bilal's face, hardly seeing him. His hand involuntarily releases the bag and it falls to the floor with a small crash. Bea stirs, and her eyes swimming open and focus on his face.

JULIA

Bea!

BEA
(weak and hoarse)

Hello, Bilal.

INT. BANK. DAY

Julia is at the bank counter. Bea and Lucy stand on either side of her. Julia puts her face to her hands.

JULIA

No. That can't be possible.

The little bank clerk looks up from his desk.

CLERK

I am sorry, madam. This is the Moroccan postal service and anything is possible.

INT. HOTEL. DAY

Back in the room, Bilal stands at the end of the mattress. Behind him, his big uniform is draped on the wall. He looks at Bea and she views him silently through feverishly large, dark eyes. He kneels beside her, stroking her hair. He puts a hand behind her ear.

BILAL

What's this?

With a little flourish, he removes the large jewel that usually fastens his turban. He turns it in front of her face. Bea watches it, then looks up with a faint smile

132

No. It's for you. To keep.

Bea awkwardly frees her hand from under the bedcovers and takes the brooch. Jewel and hand disappear again under the sheets. When she talks, it's in a very quiet whisper.

BEA

So you're going to leave again, aren't you?

BILAL

No . . .

BEA

Bilal? Is Lucy really your little girl now?

BILAL

No.

He looks down at her, disquiet on his face.

You both are.

BEA

Even if you heard things?

BILAL

Things?

BEA

Would I still be your little girl?

BILAL

But you must do something first.

He puts his hand on her head and smiles down at her.

You sleep now . . .

BEA

Bilal? You'll remember to take care of Lucy, won't you?

Bilal looks back at her, a little startled.

BILAL

Yes. Of course.

Bea closes her eyes, but not before she peeps up at him and sees his cheeks are running with tears.

Of course.

EXT. CITY SQUARE. NIGHT

Crowds and their faces, disparate music, lantern light, smoke. Eyes watchful, Bilal moves through the crowd. Finally, he finds his objective. Aziz and Isham move through the café tables selling loose cigarettes from a Winston cartoon. The two boys are laughing and relaxed.

BILAL

Aziz!

INT. HOTEL ROOM. DAWN

Julia and the two girls are asleep on the same mattress. The door opens silently and Bilal slips into the room with cat-like stealth. He removes his sword and outfit from where they hang on the wall by the door and, with a quick glance at the sleeping girls, makes to exit. But a second look shows him that Bea is awake and watching. He raises a finger to his lips, smiles and slips away. Back on the mattress, Bea lies with her eyes open, thoughtful and alert.

INT. HOTEL. DAY

Julia wakes to see Lucy and Bea seated at the end of the mattress. Bea is wearing a white turban on which Bilal's big brooch has been fixed. They smile at her.

JULIA

Where did you get that?

BEA

Bilal gave it to me.

JULIA

That was kind of him.

She rises and moves towards the door. She notices the void where Bilal's uniform was.

Where's Bilal's outfit?

She turns to the girls.

Have you seen Bilal's outfit?

Realization dawns.

Oh, my God. No . . . He's done it again.

The girls watch her.

How could he do that?

LUCY

Has Bilal gone back to Agadir?

JULIA

No, darling. He's vanished again.

INT. HOTEL. DAY

A different hotel room in the Medina, quite plushly furnished. A full-length mirror hangs there and in the reflection stands a pale, bearded middle-aged German man. He does a little turn and watches himself admiringly. Complete with turban and scimitar, he is dressed from head to toe in Bilal's Berber outfit. The sword is out of its sheath. Affecting a kind of pantomime posture, he scrutinizes himself, eyes narrowed.

GERMAN
(*to himself*)

Ja . . . Neat . . .

The man turns to where Bilal, Aziz and Isham are squatting together on the low bed. They look up at him.

136

BILAL

Two thousand dirham.

The man chuckles to himself.

GERMAN

Oh, sure. So shall we start at two hundred?

Bilal and the two boys stare at him. They are trying to look like three sullen street-toughs, but you can see it in their eyes: they're beaten, even before they begin.

EXT. STREET. EVENING

Bilal and the two boys are outside in the street now. Early evening. An overwhelming level of traffic noise. Aziz's face is full of scarcely repressed fury. Conversation in Arabic.

AZIZ

Write me a letter, Bilal.

BILAL
(*smiling*)

A letter? What kind of letter?

AZIZ

From very, very far away.

He looks into his friend's face.

Because that is where you must go. If you follow this madness.

Bilal watches as the two boys move off.

B'slema.

ISHAM
(*stops and turns*)

God will protect you, Bilal.

He smiles at Bilal faintly and runs to catch up with his friend.

INT. TICKET OFFICE. DAY

A ticket clerk behind a counter. Behind him, a dog-eared travel poster showing a dreary public monument; written underneath is the name ZAGREB. *The dialogue is in French.*

> CLERK

Your passport, please.

Now we see Bilal at the counter, money in hand. He casts a glance round in despair.

> BILAL

Passport?

> CLERK

I cannot issue these tickets without a passport and a visa. It is the law.

He glances up at Bilal.

You do have a passport, my friend?

Bilal looks back at him, his face long with despair.

> BILAL

And what of charity? To strangers? Is that not also the law?

> CLERK

That is the law of the Koran. Yes.

Bilal leans into the counter, a face hard as flint.

> BILAL

Then listen to me . . .

INT. HOTEL COURTYARD. DAY

Lucy runs through the courtyard and approaches Julia with three identical envelopes in her hands.

> LUCY

Mum, there's some letters.

Julia takes and opens them. Her face darkens into a frown.

Is it the cheque?

JULIA

No. It's three tickets to London . . .

LUCY

From Dad?

JULIA

I suppose so. Though I can't see how. I can't see how at all.

She glances round.

Something strange is going on here.

Lucy looks up at her with concern on her face.

Well, at least we can get home. I suppose. If we want to.

She looks down at Lucy's worried face.

EXT. SQUARE. NIGHT

Julia, the two girls and Eva are seated at an outdoor café. Julia sees Aziz in the crowd and rushes out to talk to him. The others watch. Now Julia returns, her face thoughtful and her footsteps slow.

EVA

So, what new mystery?

JULIA

Bilal's gone to Casablanca. He wants to become an architect.

Eva looks at her for a moment, then breaks into a peal of laughter.

Actually, he's in serious trouble, I'm sure of it. We have to help.

EVA

Bilal's gone, Julia. He's gone for ever. That's just how is it.

JULIA

Exactly what do you know?

EVA

Only – the journey's over, Julia.

LUCY

Mum . . .

EVA

Use the tickets, Julia.

Lucy gives Julia's sleeve a big tug.

LUCY

Mum, Bea's *crying*.

JULIA

What?

Julia looks in Bea's direction, then stands.

Bea.

The three of them approach where Bea sits at her table, her head down, sobbing. Julia puts a hand on her shoulder.

Bea, what's wrong?

Bea looks up and wipes her face, sniffing.

BEA

If we leave tomorrow, does that mean we'll never come back?

Julia throws Eva an incredulous look.

JULIA

Of course not, darling.

Eva sits on the chair next to Bea and unveils her face.

EVA

You can keep a secret, can't you?

Bea nods.

Do you see that group of stars?

Bea looks up at the sky with her wet face.

That's the seven brothers of the Prophet. If you make a wish on them, it's bound to come true.

Bea scrutinizes Eva's eyes.

                              BEA
All right then.

The two women and Lucy watch as Bea faces the night sky and inaudibly talks to the stars in a speech full of sniffs, muttered promises and avowals.

EXT. MARRAKECH. DAY

Early morning now and the long, slow train of Berber horsemen moves in single file down the deserted street. Lucy stands motionless on the pavement and watches as, one by one, their faces pass, towering over her, each beneath its jewel and turban: aloof, possessed of mystery; or dark and slightly sly; or innocent, young and full of dreams. To Lucy's eyes, a slow procession of Moroccan faces.

They pass, and the sounds of hoofs and bridle bells move off into the distance. Lucy looks around. Bea and Julia are waiting for her some way off, beneath the big arch of the city wall. The tartan dufflebag lies between them.

INT. TRAIN. DAY

Julia and the girls move into the train compartment. Finding their seats, they heave the big dufflebag on to the luggage rack. They settle and Bea closes her eyes, while Lucy bites into the rind of an orange.

A whistle blows. The train moves off. They sit and watch the platform move beneath them. *Again and again, the platform signs say* MARRAKECH, MARRAKECH. *The train picks up speed.*

Suddenly from the platform, a face briefly crosses the window, his eyes in theirs. Lucy leaps to her feet.

LUCY

Bilal!!!

Julia leaps to her feet.

Pulling down the window. They all lean out.

But he is nowhere to be seen. There is only the train station as it recedes into the distance.

INT. TRAIN. NIGHT

The two children are asleep in the luggage racks. Julia sits alone, smoking a skinny roll-up, her face reflected against the passing darkness, concern on it. A sigh and a long exhalation of smoke.

JULIA

Oh, Bilal . . .

She looks up. There is Lucy's face peering down at her, nose and chin protruding through the string netting. Their eyes meet.

A distant sound attracts their attention – a persistent, frantic honking of a vehicle horn. Julia looks out of the window and her brow knits into a frown. The girls clamber down from the luggage racks.

Now their faces are at the window. A pick-up truck is speeding alongside the train. At the back of that, some goats and chickens bleat and cluck in alarm. In the cabin, a man in a red turban leans waving out of the window, his other hand on the wheel.

The truck kicks up a funnel of dust as the man unwinds his turban. Back on the train, their eyes widen with astonishment. Julia pulls down the window. They lean out. It is Bilal.

With his free hand, he holds the end of the red turban cloth, which flies behind him like a flickering scarlet banner. A laugh convulses his face.

BILAL

Hideous Kinky!!

BEA and JULIA

Hideous Kinky!!

Now train and truck veer apart.

BILAL
(already distant)

Hideous Kinky!!

The three faces veer away as the train curves into a landscape of palms and the truck continues – turban flying – on its solitary, distant path into – wherever.

Now we hold on Bea. Her eyes close tight. Her chest fills with air.

BEA

Beee Laaaaal!!!

Everything vanishes to dust, and landscape, and the sun's last light.

Music up.

Credits

147

CREW

Director	Gillies MacKinnon
Screenplay	Billy MacKinnon
Producer	Ann Scott
Executive Producers	Mark Shivas, Simon Relph
Co-Producers	Emmanuel Schlumberger,
	Annabel Karouby,
	Marina Gefter
Line Producer	Paul Sarony
Casting	Susie Figgis
Sound Recordist	Bruno Charier
Costume Designer	Kate Carin
Production Designers	Louise Marzaroli,
	Pierre Gompertz
Music	John Keane
Editor	Pia Di Ciaula
Director of Photography	John de Borman, BSC
1st Assistant Directors	Stephen Woolfenden,
	Mohamed Nesrate
2nd Assistant Director	Beni Turkson
3rd Assistant Directors	Larbi Idrissi, Jim Threapleton,
	Abdelwahab Adil
Line Producer (France)	Pierre Sayag
Production Managers	Hilary Benson, Omar Jawal
Production Coordinators	Ann Lynch, Khadija Alami
Producers' Assistants	Clare Oliver, Alix Raynaud
Script Editor	Stephanie Guerrasio
Script Supervisor	Susanna Lenton
Make-up and Hair Designer	Mel Gibson
Make-up Artist	Lesa Warrener
Make-up Assistant	Khalid Alami
Make-up Dailies	Alison Munn,
	Majdouline Rimmel
Wardrobe Master	John Norster
Wardrobe Assistant	Margie Fortune
Casting (France)	Juliette Menager
Casting Assistant (Morocco)	Ahmed Abounouom
Focus Puller	Chyna Thomson
Clapper Loader	Ros Ellis

Grip	Robin Stone
Camera Trainee	Joshua Lee
Grip Trainee	Jaber Jaafar
Camera Labour	Youssef Taoufik,
	My Mustapha Elidrissi
2nd Unit Director	Billy MacKinnon
Steadicam Operator	Alastair Rae
2nd Focus Puller	Lorna Will
Stunt Coordinator	Stuart St Paul
Boom Operator	Jean-Marie Blondel
Sound Trainee	Said Ghounaim
Art Director	Jon Henson
Assistant Art Directors	Hadj Lahcen Kahia,
	Lucy Reeves
Set Dresser	Cristina Casali
Property Master	Mike Malik
Property Buyer UK	Fran Cooper
Assistant Property Buyer	Said El Kounti
Dressing Props	Mustapha Haouas,
	Miloud El Kanaoui
Construction Manager	Mark Pritchard
Stand-by Carpenter	Christopher Higson
Carpenter	Mustapha Benkiram
Stand-by Riggers	Richard Stone, Lahcen Herraf
Location Manager	Hassan Bajja
Location Assistants	Driss Benchhiba,
	Abderrahim Taha
Crowd Marshal	Mustapha Fathi
Gaffer	Steve Kitchen
Best Boy	Andy Curling
Generator Operators	Brandan Evans,
	Azeddine Mazile
Electricians	Abdellilah Laghrissi,
	Habib Bensalem
Trainee Electricians	My Youssef Taoufik,
	Said Lagbouri
Electrical Labour	Tahar Ajoualil,
	Kibire Charkaoui
1st Assistant Editor	James Lingard

Post-Production Supervisor	Alistair Hopkins
Music Consultant	Liz Gallacher
Dubbing Mixer	Tim Alban
Dubbing Assistant	Hugh Johnson
Supervising Sound Editor	Zane Hayward
Dialogue Editor	Stewart Henderson
Foley Editor	Anthony Faust
ADR Editor	Dave McGrath
Conform Editors	Gavin Buckley, Gabby Smith, Giles Gardner
FT2 Assistant Trainees	Emile Bradshaw, Tayo Awoniyi
Foley Artists	Jack Stew, Felicity Cottrell
Loop Group	Brendan Donnison
Drivers	Abdelilah Hamsaoui, Mounim Hajjam, Abdellatif Faraj, Mustapha Bendari, Noureddine Benchhiba, Amine Jibari, Lahcen Khouya, Abdessamad Bounagui
Camera Car	Chris Weightman
Make-up Truck	Graham Cheetham
Wardrobe Truck	Alan Lewandowski
Lighting	El Wafi Hassani
Forward Construction	Ahmed Ghounaim
Caravans & Minibus	Larbi Ben Bella, Hussein Larbi
Tracking Vehicle	Paul Rosevear
Catering by	Location Café
Caterers	Andy Aldridge, Colin Stredwick, Richard Corfield
Tea Boy	Brahim Boukili El Hassani
Stills Photographer	Sophie Baker
Unit Publicist	Linda Gamble
Publicity	MacDonald & Rutter
Chaperones	Catherine Amesbury, Anna Ritchie
Tutors	Barry Marsdon, Khalil Boulahcen
Unit Nurse	Hakima Hammoudi
Stand-ins	Fatiha Farsani,

	Housseine El Demlak,
	Afraa Steila, Nadia El Fatima,
	Dounia Chirat
Assistant to Director	Soumaya Bellafquih
Assistant to Kate Winslet	Amanda Scott
Production Runner	Aziz Hamichi
Production Secretaries	Ian Buchan, Fatima Benrahma
Production Accountant	Jim Hajicosta
Assistant Accountant	Richard Wood
Accountant (France)	Martine Bourdon
Cashier	Mohamed Rachid Alami
Accounts Assistant	Darmouch Hafid
Completion Guarantor	Film Finances Ltd
Banking Finance	Cofiloisirs,
	Entente Distribution Ltd
Insurance provided by	Media Insurance Brokers Ltd
Shipping Services	Renown Freight Ltd
Facilities Vehicles	Filmflow Ltd
Motion Picture Film	KODAK
Camera & Lenses	Movietech Camera Rental Ltd
Lighting Equipment	AFM Lighting Ltd
Laboratory	Rank Film Laboratories
Neg Cutting	Tru-Cut
Titles Design	Plume Ltd
Titles and Opticals	General Screen Enterprises
Sound Recording	Videosonics
Post Production at	Goldcrest Post Production
Music Recorded at	Angel Studios

Singer/Guitar player – Rais El Housseine Bou-El-Masseil
Ney player – Kudsi Erguner
Musicians of the London Pops Orchestra

'On the Road Again'
Written by A. Wilson/F. Jones
Published by EMI United Partnership Ltd
Performed by Canned Heat
Courtesy of EMI Records

'Here Comes the Sun'
Written by George Harrison
© 1969 Harrisongs Limited
Performed by Richie Havens
Courtesy of Polydor Records Inc.
Licensed by kind permission of the
PolyGram Commercial Marketing Division

'Alone Again Or'
Written by Bryan MacLean
© Embassy Music Corp USA
Licensed by Campbell Connely & Co. Ltd, London
Performed by Love
Courtesy of Elektra Entertainment Group
By Arrangement with Warner Special Products/
Warner Music UK Ltd

'Worlds They Rise and Fall'
Written by Mike Heron
© 1971 Warlock Music Limited
Performed by The Incredible String Band
Courtesy of Island Records Limited
Licensed by kind permission of
PolyGram Commercial Marketing Division

'Baba Baba Mektoubi'
Performed by Jil Jilala
Courtesy of Société d'Edition Hassania, Morocco

'Road'
Written by Nick Drake
© 1972 Warlock Music Limited
Performed by Nick Drake
Courtesy of Island Records Limited
Licensed by kind permission of the
PolyGram Commercial Marketing Division

'The Tortoise's Song'
Arranged by Ishteeb Laggari
Performed by Khalifa Ould Eide and Dimi Mint Abba
by kind permission of World Circuit Records

'You Don't Have to Cry'
Composed by Stephen Stills
Published by Almo Music Corp./Gold Hill Music Inc.
Performed by Crosby, Stills & Nash
Courtesy of Atlantic Recording Corp.
By Arrangement with Warner Special Products/
Warner Music UK Ltd

Sufi quotes from *Mystical Dimensions of Islam*
by Annemarie Schimmel.
Copyright © 1975 by the University of North Carolina Press.
Used by permission of the publisher. All right reserved.

Consultant on Sufism   Hoda Mohajerani

Special thanks to:

Vincent Malle, Bernardine Coverley, Kate Wilson,
Colin Vaines, Sophie Dix, William Hinshelwood,
Geoffrey Paget, Jane Aresti, Gretta Finer, Sarah Atkinson,
Jane Loveless, Mustapha Sbia

Centre Cinématographique Marocain
and the people of Marrakech

A British / French Co-Production

Developed with the assistance of BBC Films

Greenpoint Films

and with the support of
The European Script Fund
an initiative of the MEDIA programme of the
European Union

Supported by the National Lottery
through the Arts Council of England